Living a Narrative Life

ESSAYS ON THE POWER OF STORIES

KEITH HERRON

Smyth & Helwys Publishing, Inc.
6316 Peake Road
Macon, Georgia 31210-3960
1-800-747-3016
©2019 by Keith Herron
All rights reserved.

Library of Congress Cataloging-in-Publication Data

Names: Herron, Keith, author.
Title: Living a narrative life : essays exploring the power of stories / by
Keith Herron.
Description: Macon : Smyth & Helwys, 2018. | Includes bibliographical
references and index.
Identifiers: LCCN 2018042387 | ISBN 9781641730907 (pbk. : alk. paper)
Subjects: LCSH: Life cycle, Human. | Storytelling.
Classification: LCC HQ519 .H47 2018 | DDC 808.8/03561--dc23
LC record available at https://lccn.loc.gov/2018042387

This book is dedicated to all those in my prologue portrait.
As a sign of living across my own arc,
most of them are long passed and
lying in their appointed places in the
Cottage Hill Cemetery in North Texas.

I also dedicate this to Wanda, my companion and co-traveler in life.

Contents

I Am–*Egō Eimi*

The Foundation for Living a Storied Life

The ancients knew about the power of identity, the power of a person knowing who they are, and the power of the self. Without having a science called psychology to describe their thinking, they were still able to identify their essential and central self by referring to themselves as "I am." The phrase "I am" has great power, and its place in everyday thought is a powerful reminder how a person may make a definitive and undeniable claim to their existence.

I am not an etymologist, a philologist, or a linguist, but I did take Greek in postgraduate studies. Admittedly, I'm a casual interpreter at best, but I have enough tools to know where to look for more depth about words in Koine (biblical) Greek. For a working knowledge about yourself, or your "self," we should consider how the ancient Greeks talked about these things. They used a particular term for "I am"—*egō eimi* (first person singular, present tense of the verb "to be")—to signify that an individual could embrace a sense of self. *Egō eimi* (/eh-GO ee-MEE/) was a familiar phrase people used to identify themselves to others, to claim simply, "I am" or "I exist."

In common speech, "I am" can be a simple way to respond, "It is I" or "I am the one," but there is a deeper meaning to the phrase. This claim is the beginning of developing an interior self. It's widely known we develop the main structure of our personality in our earliest stages of childhood, but beyond that, children are also learning to recognize their sense of self. "I am" is a prelude to also learning "you are." In our interpersonal relationships, "I am" is not sufficient for healthy growth until we also learn "you are." In infancy, the child does not see these distinctions but lives in a merged world. Thus, our growth pushes us to recognize where "I am" meets the boundary of where "you are."

Egō eimi, "I am," is a subject (I) and linking verb (am) that precedes a predicate nominative, the part of a sentence or clause that clarifies or renames the subject. The linking verb in a sentence with a predicate nominative can be replaced by "equals." Thus, "I am the author of this book" could be understood as "I = author of this book." There are many ways the predicate nominative is used in everyday speech. Some common ways are (1) as an introduction answering the question, "Who are you?" to which I would say, "I am *Keith*"; (2) as a qualifier answering the question, "What are you?" to which I might say, "I am a *Chiefs fan*"; (3) as an identifier in response to someone seeking to know how I identify with another person or thing, as when I say "I am *Don and Kevin's favorite brother*"; (4) as a differentiator in response to someone seeking to know how to recognize me by asking, "Who is the one who . . . ?" to which I would respond, "It is *I*."

Before Descartes made his statement, "*cogito, ergo sum*"—"I think, therefore I am"—the Hebrews were exploring the Saudi deserts and following the God whose preferred name was "I AM." When Moses questions the likelihood that the Egyptian Pharaoh will ask him, "Who sent you?" God answers, "Tell him, 'I AM' has sent you." This assertion of identity of self, divine or human, always begins with the individual's recognition of their existence. It is a basic yet profound affirmation of self that one can assert as a reason for being. One of the challenges of seeking maturity is finding this truth for oneself and creating a center of existence derived from the confidence it provides.

Jesus used the phrase *egō eimi* in metaphors: I am . . . *the way, the truth, and the life*; I am . . . *the bread of life*; I am . . . *the light*; I am . . . *the door*; I am . . . *the good shepherd*; I am . . . *the resurrection and the life*; I am . . . *the vine*. In the Gospel of John, these are known as the seven *egō eimi* (I am) teachings that use predicate nominatives as Jesus' way of making self-statements to his followers.

Exploring the All-inclusive "I Am"

If you are part of a narrative group that gathers to deepen your understanding of your lives, consider using this section at the end of each essay as a guide to help you and your group hold meaningful sessions where you share your stories. Story starters are meant to provide handles to guide your group in discussing the issues raised in each essay.

Each stage-of-life essay that follows is introduced by first-person material meant to describe what it's like to inhabit that age and also to suggest the concerns one may face during that stage. This section is printed in italics to separate it from the issue-driven commentary in each essay. It is a description, a sampler, a confession of sorts to help readers remember their own stories of that stage or imagine the journey ahead in stages yet to be experienced.

As we begin, please know that

I am *the one wishing you clarity and courage as you explore your stories.*
I am *the one hoping you will find friends with whom to share the journey of discovery.*
I am *the one believing you will be enriched and your life's story deepened.*

How to Use This Book

We hold our stories in the vault of our memories, and we interpret their meaning largely on our own. But in narrative thought, no single meaning is the only meaning, and it's likely that most of our stories are not our stories alone; they are shared by others. The other characters in these memories have their own versions and interpretations of our shared stories, and exploring together those versions only deepens their meanings. However, my version of a shared story can be so different from someone else's that we might question whether we can claim it as "shared." Realizing that the "facts" of our memories can be fuzzy, thickening the story with the perspectives gleaned from others helps us gain new insights about ourselves and about the meaning of what we have experienced.

Studies in Memory

Our stories are the on-ramps to creating community because they give us something to talk about together. We talk about what has happened in life, and we talk about how those experiences have shaped and molded us. We talk about what the stories mean as guides to knowing ourselves at a deeper level. Stories help us find meaning when we explore them with curiosity. By telling my story, I tap into the universal story that all of us experience, and I may help stimulate you to remember your own stories across the arc of life. A common human experience, no matter one's language, culture, race, education level, or economic level, means that we all live on a map plotted by the arc of life. We live storied lives because our journey across time is composed of the vignettes of human experiences that we receive in the contract of our creation. The gift of the universe is that we are granted existence, and from that we take one step after another along the arc of life. Our stories, while individual and unique, are also communal and common.

Once you go down this path of assessing your life through its stories, you will become an expert in the life experiences that have been lived in the course of time. The accoutrements change, but the structures and settings in which we live our stories are amazingly, eerily similar across time and culture. We are often mesmerized by the stories of others from different times and vastly different cultures that draw us in as if our own story is being told. We can tap into the universal power of stories by welcoming our own stories that bubble up from wherever they are stored.

We don't live neatly described narratives, but we retain the memories of our experiences in narrative structures. The lived experiences of your stories likely don't have clear boundaries marking the beginning, middle, and end, and each story likely overlaps other stories. One of the functions of memory, though, is that the stories sort themselves out and take on a stricter narrative structure, so we retain our experiences in story formats. Our experiences may be like a big box of crayons left in the car in the heat of summer, where all the colors melt into a hot, sloppy mess of color, but somehow we store them as narratives structured by meaning, edited and packaged for retention. We retain our experiences as vignettes as a way of creating meaning.

The narrative process I describe in this book is an intentional way of exploring our stories that can be done alone or in groups designed to follow a narrative process. This approach is durable, and the principles of narrative work can be applied individually as far as one is willing to venture. But the principles can also be adopted by a small group of friends, a book club, or any gathering of others who wish to explore their stories in the safety and security of a covenanted group.

Exploring Your Stories Alone

Alone, you can start by selecting a handful of stories to recall in depth. Stories that linger in your thoughts and mark important occasions can be a beginning point. My teaching partner, Steve, explores his stories on his own. He begins by writing down a simple version of his story. There is no polish to this beginning step, and one should never assume that this beginning is finished. Allow time and creativity to put down on paper the basic outline of the story. Recall as much of the setting as possible, and try to include as much detail as you can remember.

Write a draft of the story and include the story's facts as widely as you can remember them, but also try to include any confusing aspects, important interactions you might have had with others, or even the ways you experienced the story in the moment as emotionally complicated. Pay attention to the elements that animate the story in your memory. See yourself, see others, and observe how the story follows a narrative structure. Focus on the part of the story that particularly attracts you to it. Be alert for elements that are confusing to you, even after the story has receded into the past. Some stories are laden with conflict that makes it difficult to identify their meaning. Problem-laden stories can be taxing, and they may even be stories of regret or shame. There's no one age when these stories may occur, but it's not hard to recognize them in childhood, adolescence, or the early stages of adulthood. Some of these stories are well beyond our ability to fix them, so they may linger in memory as troublesome.

Try to capture each story as closely as possible, and then set it aside long enough to let it settle. The Tao Te Ching asks, "Do you have the patience to wait till your mud settles and your water becomes clear? Can you remain unmoving till the right action arises in itself?"[1]

The goal is to allow the story to thicken. In exploring our stories, we never tell the full extent of each one in a single telling. There are always unexamined aspects that have been ignored or left out. The unexamined material is rich with new implications. Think of the colorizing of black and white movies. All is essentially the same, but there are new ways in which to experience them. In a similar way, stories become clearer when we allow them to mature. Writing the first draft gets the mainframe of the story in place, but the additional details helps us explore the deeper meaning.

Once you choose a story and write a first draft, try to give the story a headline that will begin to shape how you understand its meaning. This is the first step toward understanding how the story illuminates your life. The headline is also a handle by which you can affiliate with the story.

Here are two stories, both illustrating life experiences in my adolescence of who I would be as a leader. In each one, I demonstrated innately how I would respond to life as it was lived and who I would be in response to life's possibilities.

For three summers in high school and early college, I worked for the Dr. Pepper Bottling Company in Dallas. The first summer, I worked on the sales trucks as they headed out in the dawning moments of the day. We would load the trucks as to the expected needs of customers on the day's route. My memories of working with sales drivers are decidedly positive, but the next two summers I worked in the bottling plant, where the process of filling Dr. Pepper bottles in all its many flavors continued twenty-four hours a day. The company depended on the massive summer sales to sustain the business.

In the bottling plant, we worked from sundown to sunup in the nighttime heat where the only relief came during an occasional break, the mealtime just after midnight, or a rare mechanical breakdown. It was repetitive and very physical work as we slung wooden cases of empty or full bottles that had come off the fleet of trucks. Empty bottles were run through the enormous washing machine that cleaned them by the hundreds in a never-ending process that went as fast as the empties could be loaded. Clean bottles continued along the never-stopping assembly line to the filling stations, where they were filled and capped. These recycled full bottles were then dropped into cases and ready to be loaded by forklifts onto the delivery trucks.

Every few days someone would quit. The management filled out a crew at the beginning of the summer but didn't replenish the crews to sustain the process. By mid-summer, I approached the manager of the night shift, inquiring why we were so depleted. Those who remained were challenged to keep up with the activity of servicing the cleaning and filling of thousands of bottles as if a full crew was present. My inquiry did not generate new employees to give us the minimum number of workers needed, and it became apparent the reduced work force was expected to keep everything in motion. In my frustration, one night I organized a walkout by those of us who were working. When a group of us walked out after the first break, the plant was forced to stop the lines that night. What happened after that is a mystery to me. Did they bring in replacement workers the next night? I don't know. While I was acting under a principled notion of an agreement to serve the company as an employee, I acted impetuously and undermined the operation.

I learned a great number of lessons about myself at this time in my life, about my life as an employee, and about the nature of working for a company that was focused solely on putting out their product with the highest efficiency, no matter how the employees were treated. In thinking about my story, I'm forced to consider how the themes of work and commitment have played out in my life in other settings, particularly now that I serve as the leader of an organization with a large staff that likewise deals with the delicate balance of give and take as employees.

It was obvious that I was developing a personal understanding of the code of ethics that I would follow in my life as an employee. I was also adopting a commitment of working hard, albeit with limits as to how hard I would work and under what conditions that work would be done. Looking back, I see that my actions were irresponsible. I recruited others to adopt my own response to the work conditions rather than following my convictions alone. This was an early indication of my leadership but also cautionary as to the kind of leader I would become. If I were to write a headline for this story, I'd call it "An Irresponsible Leader Emerges, Company Suffers."

Next, here's an example from my early teen years as a Boy Scout. In this story, I must have been twelve or thirteen years old, and my Scout troop was camping along a creek that ran through a rural farm owned by one of my classmates. That farmer (or my classmate, his daughter) is not significant to this story other than it's how I frame the location of what happened. Remembering the farm allows me to locate the story in time and space. The story I remember is populated with friends I can still recall and with the adult Scout leaders, who were vitally involved in our Scouting experience.

My best friend at the time was David, and we were friends in school and lived down the same street from one another. David and I were off in the woods looking for firewood for the camp. Much of the Scouting life involves campfires, and the need for good firewood was always a part of our weekend camp-outs. With an ax in hand, we came across a dead tree that was still standing. It had long ago died but still stood strong, even though it was stripped of leaves and bark. No matter that the tree was too big for our need for firewood—in our minds, we determined to cut it down. If we had succeeded, what would we then do, as the tree was too big for any firewood needs we could supply? None of that seemed to make sense to us, and we both took turns chopping on the tree, using the skills we had been taught about swinging an ax with our feet spread apart at the width of our shoulders and perpendicular to the cut we wanted to make. We had been taught to chop down at a 45-degree angle, then alternate with a cut from below at the opposing angle to form a V. Each of us swung until tired, and then the other would take over. All of this went as we were taught, and both of us used good form.

The tree, however, was not green and was very hard. David swung hard downward at the prescribed 45-degree angle and the ax, rather than cutting into the wood, glanced off the tree's hardness and buried itself in David's left foot, the one directly next to the tree. As gory as that might sound, it took a moment for either of us to see this tragedy for what it was. David's face was frozen for a few seconds until he realized how awful this was. Then he began screaming, and I helped him get down on the ground. From here, the story is muddled. I don't remember what I did next. Did I remove the ax from his foot, or did he do that? Was there blood flowing steadily or gushing? I *might* have a memory of stripping off my T-shirt to wrap his foot to stop the bleeding. This action would have been what we had learned in first aid classes. I say I *might have* because I don't exactly recall. The memory of who did what next and how we did what we did is a blur.

I do recall running back to the camp and calling our adult leaders together. My father was one of my Scout masters, and he was among those who ran back with me to find David. By now, the whole Scout troop was awake and actively engaged with the accident. Four of us carried David by his arms and legs out of the woods to someone's waiting car. Somehow I ended up being the one Scout in the car to take David to the hospital located a short drive away.

From there we entered the emergency room, and doctors and nurses took over. David's surgeon pieced him back together again, doing the corrective work of dealing with the many sliced bones in his foot, the nerves, tendons, muscles, and severed arteries. I stayed at the hospital until David was taken to a room.

While the experience is seared into my memory, making meaning of it has been limited because, at the time, I could only see the primal nature of the injury and could not see myself clearly. The meaning of this story, however, was shared between my father and me in the after beyond that moment, through the years that led up to my father's death. In the time after this event, my friendship with David waned as we engaged in different activities with different friends in high school. I don't recall talking together about this seminal moment in which he was injured and I was involved in tending to his injury and mustering the resources of our troop to respond. What I do remember are the conversations my father and I occasionally had. In adulthood, I have recalled this story of an ax and a severe injury mostly through my father's eyes. The story from my own eyes was limited to seeing everything happen in the blink of an eye and, in the moments that followed, to dealing with my friend's intense pain of having nearly cut his foot off with an ax. The lens taking all this in was limited in experience but seemed focused on David, the ax and the tree, the blow of the ax ricocheting off the hardened tree, the horrific gash, and David's panic and the flood of searing pain. I can see all of this, but I cannot see myself other than through the lens of my own eyes. I'm an actor in this story, but I cannot see myself. I can see everything unfold, what happened to David, the urgency in which I called the troop together, the actions we took to carry him out of the woods and into a car that delivered him to the emergency room, but I cannot see the me who responded in the moment.

The lens of my father's viewpoint, however, was different, as the story he saw unfolding included me and how I responded. He was in the group of people who came running in response to the accident. He was part of the decisions that were made to both tend to David using emergency first aid and to take him to the nearest hospital. My father's experience of this included me, the first wave of help, the one who rallied the troop to respond, and my direct involvement in both first aid and in seeing that David was taken to the hospital.

Over the years, my father has made it clear to me that my actions were pivotal to David's well-being. I won't say heroic, because I don't think anything I did was heroic. In my father's telling of the story over the many years that followed this event, he made plain to me that when a moment of testing came along, I was ready, that I made the correct responses using the training I had already received and giving direction to the troop, adults and boys alike, in acting strategically in the crisis of this bloody accident. My father always retold this story affirming my cool-headedness and my leadership in the moment.

The headline I've given this story? "In Crisis, a Leader Emerges." The lens of the story follows David and his injury, but the meaning is found in how I acted in response to the event. I'm sure David's headline for this same event would not include me or my actions. The headline was taken from my father's view of the event. From that day's events, he used this story as an example of the leadership that Scouting aimed to teach boys like me. While I value my father's retelling of the story, I realize that the events of that day were equally important to each of us.

Over the years, Steve and I have led groups of clergy and other leaders in exploring their stories of leadership. We have used a narrative process described in the book by Richard Hester and Kelly Walker-Jones, *Know Your Story and Lead with It*, which guides leaders in exploring the narratives that shaped and molded their leadership skills. Using a group process, participants are asked to respond to a series of leadership topics in exploring key issues for leaders. One of those topics is "Tell a leadership story about you before the age of 20." Leaders don't come from thin air. Leaders emerge in response to the living of life. They are people who don't decide to be leaders but merely live into their own lives and lead.

The story of that crisis in the woods is one in a sequence of other stories when I wasn't thinking about becoming a leader, but my father's observation shined a light on the crisis that I did not realize until I saw the event through his eyes. In this single circumstance, my father and I became a covenanted community by daring to relive the story, both from my own memory and also from his memory.

To be sure, this event was not my story alone. But neither was it merely David's story. Both of us were engaged completely in this tragic accident together, but even then it was a story shared by everyone there. To be honest, David, wherever he might be today, may not remember me by name or importance to his personal crisis, nor would he likely remember much else other than how significant the accident was to him personally.

Narratives are often communal narratives, and we are forced to embrace that any single story has multiple meanings. For my own meaning, I have the richness of my father's memory to help me thicken the story. This is a story I recall in responding to "Tell a story of leadership before the age of 20." This single story is not a complete or thorough rendering of the challenge of seeing how leadership has emerged in me, but it's illustrative of other forces at work in my adolescence that gave meaning to how my early stories molded my later experiences in life.

Taken together, from my summer work at the soft drink company and this experience as a Boy Scout, I have two vignettes that give me some notion of the leader I was becoming, both positively and negatively. Telling one story alone gives one outcome, but holding both stories in balance, I can see the fault lines and the rich possibilities of how I was growing and developing as a person and as a leader.

To use a narrative process, one works with intent in telling a version of the story that seems honest and complete. A first telling of the story is never considered a deep version, even if the facts of the story are complete. One should consider that one's memory is limited and that none of us has complete recall. In isolation, one might go to others who were active in the story to consider how others might tell it differently. To challenge one's own story with the perspective of others can be illuminating. Any differences in how the story is observed can serve to open up the story for new meaning. One can see one's own stories from someone else's vantage point and perhaps gain important new insights to be considered.

This solo approach to exploring your stories is not random, although many might gain significant insights into themselves by accepting the stories that memory delivers to them for consideration. Rather, this is a structured approach to latch on to the universal stories that we all seem to live out in our own unique ways. Particularly, if you happen to have a narrative group of friends who have agreed to explore their lives, a structured approach will shape a shared experience that will be both unique and common. There are universal experiences that we can all describe: for example, your first experience of being lost, of realizing your parents are not all-knowing, or of facing your first failure or loss. Because they are universal, these types of stories are referred to as *archetypal*. They transcend differences and bring people together in shared experience.

Developing a Narrative Group

A group of people who wish to explore their stories together can provide an amazing experience of community. People can gather with purpose to share their stories, or an existing group like a book club can adopt a narrative process to explore stories together. My experience in group work would suggest that groups of four to five are optimal because of the nature of how the group shares. With larger groups, time to share is limited and there is less possibility that all members can stay involved. Attendance is important, as stories build from meeting to meeting. Active listeners must be present in order to experience the stories together. Once you have a few interested people, decide on the place, time, and frequency to meet. It may be helpful for each person to have a copy of this book.

A Narrative Principles Toolkit

The theoretical support for this collection of essays is derived from narrative psychology, a model dedicated to helping people explore their life stories for deeper meaning. Narrative therapy is an expression of narrative psychology and an offshoot of a larger field of practice known as cognitive psychology. In narrative thought, the therapist is not considered a health care professional who guides the patient in treatment as much a collaborator with the client on a mutual exploration of meaning, usually implying that the client's stories are saturated with problems that have led the client to seek help. In narrative thought, memory is essential, and there is an assumption that it is less a sure recall of what happened than the evidence of how the mind has constructed reality from an edited version of what happened. Our minds create a story version of our experiences, including a plot and a purpose that suits our unconscious need to tell a story that supports the adopted narrative of our lives. The unused snippets of the story that don't fit the plot are cut out and dropped to the editing room floor. Narrative thought nurtures curiosity about those deleted bits and seeks to understand how or why these elements were not included in the edited memory. This is where the collaboration with a therapist is attuned to the narrative of the storyteller, who is typically unconscious of the edited nature of their memories. In the collaboration together, the storyteller is allowed the possibility of rethinking the story and better understanding how it works and how it offers the possibility of a new narrative.

Tools for Groups

If you are thinking about forming a narrative study group, refer to *Know Your Story and Lead with It*, a superb aid for how people might tell their stories in a group process.[2] The work Richard Hester and Kelli Walker-Jones pioneered with clergy groups is a model that any narrative group might adapt to their purposes. Here are some additional tools for building a storytelling group. Many of the tips apply even if one is going through this process alone.

• **Commit to the process and to one another.** Make a clear commitment to engage this narrative process with purpose. Clarify the commitment. When and where will we meet? Perhaps the group could commit to a series of conversations, three to four gatherings, to give the process a chance to succeed. Groups don't need a designated leader as much as someone to serve as convener to help the group achieve its goals. This is not a model of one leading the others but of someone having the skills to call the group together and to tip over the first domino. The convener should be acquainted with the narrative process of group sharing and be willing to help the group experience the process successfully. The group members are encouraged to express themselves, establish their covenant with each other, and participate fully.

• **Develop a group covenant to create a safe atmosphere to share your stories.** Groups need a covenant of ideas that can shape the way in which they experience their stories. Such a covenant will acknowledge the value of confidentiality and full participation by all. A group covenant will help participants abide by agreements that allow them to share with confidence that their stories will be honored and respected, a trait that will allow for honesty and openness. Narrative groups should be meaningful and not constrictive or controlling, but the right structures and the group's agreement to identifiable conversation guidelines will strengthen the chance that the process will be successful and meaningful.

• **Adhere to the Parker Palmer Rules.** I recommend using what are informally called the "Parker Palmer Rules" for group conversations: *No Fixing, No Saving, No Advising, No Setting Anyone Straight.*[3] Palmer's book is aimed at groups of people who wish to share their stories with one another in ways that advocate for hearing and understanding. Palmer explores the world of shared stories and identifies the practice of healthy group intimacy. I highly recommend that his book be added to the group's library of resources to guide them toward growth and success. Palmer's chief concern is to describe a community of faith, but his principles are appropriate for any group. "No fixing, no saving, no advising, no setting each other straight" is a qualitative declaration that ensures that each member is respected and places a high value on how each person is free to explore their own story without getting bogged down with other people's advice or attempts to fix the problem. Palmer gets at the heart of why groups fail. Most of us are fixers, committed to rescuing the one who shares with us. We have advice to give in lieu of true listening. We are problem-solvers with no boundaries to allow the storyteller to fully explore the depths of a personal story. Rather than sharing a story, which likely includes elements of risk for the storyteller, a person can feel hindered by another's unabashed willingness to take over the story with their own need to intrude.

Groups that adopt these guidelines should consider posting them in the room so that when the inevitable violator drives the conversation into the ditch of telling someone what to do, the others in the group can call the violator out for their mistake. The Parker Palmer Rules purify the group's opportunity to create a safe haven in which to tell their most vulnerable stories.

• **Practice asking "not knowing" questions.** A storyteller tells their tale, and miraculously we all become expert observers. No matter the complexity of the story and the dilemma the storyteller faces, those of us who are listening seem to have all the answers. For many, this is the Achilles heel of how they relate to others. Being an outsider to the story is an intoxicating shot of hubris that allows us to presume that we can see with clarity what the storyteller cannot. This is a critical weakness for any group that has enough intimacy to allow the risk of telling a personal story but no limits to how the group can inhibit the storyteller's opportunity to find deeper meaning.

Quite simply, taking a not-knowing position is asking questions for which I don't have preconceived ideas or theories. A not-knowing position will use the language and concerns of the storyteller, allowing the possibility that new meanings might emerge. In short, I partner with the storyteller in seeking alternative stories that may come forward for consideration. The collaboration is felt when both the listener and the storyteller are involved in seeking these alternative stories.[4]

The power of taking a not-knowing position is that the nature of the conversation remains open to letting the storyteller explore new alternative meanings. This possibility is rich with hopefulness for one who is living in a problem-saturated story. Narratives are given room to thicken, deepened by the use of curious questions rather than shut down by solutions that have little meaning. Surprisingly, this not-knowing position is a form of transformative social power, discovered when the core of understanding is engaged by the freedom to think new thoughts, make new decisions, and inhabit the full range of life's possibilities. Letting go of the assumption of knowing, one must set aside the practice of analyzing a problem and rendering a solution.

Asking curious questions is at the heart of taking a not-knowing position. Curious questions acknowledge the limits of one's assumptions and stand in contrast to one's wish to fix another's story. Dick Hester and Kelli Walker-Jones offer guidelines for asking curious questions: ". . . use open-ended questions and steer clear from closed questions with only one outcome, and practice the skills of keeping the conversation open from the negative outcomes that come by violating the Parker Palmer Rules."[5]

Hester and Walker-Jones offer some examples of curious questions, which they frame as indirect questions (e.g., "I wonder how/what . . .") or as open-ended questions, which can't be answered with a simple "yes" or "no" (e.g., "What if . . . ?").

Too often, we ask leading questions that suggest there's a "right" response. As we stand outside someone else's story, there is no end to our insight; give us a problem-saturated story and we all become experts who are willing to save the storyteller from their plight. "Curious questions" help us invite reflection and move us past our need to have all the answers.

• **Seek the "relentless optimism" that supports the narrative practice.** Narrative therapy has adopted "relentless optimism" as a way to frame the narratives that are explored. This atmosphere of optimism is based on the admission that our stories may be challenging, complicated, and daunting to our sense of wholeness. Relentless optimism, then, allows for the ones who share to seek to understand their concerns with the goal of finding outcomes where growth might be experienced and a hopeful sense of maturity might come about.

When we consider our experience under the light of relentless optimism, we believe there is always another story that may surface, one that at first is not acknowledged. When we express pain or hopelessness, we can listen for shards of alternative stories, stories that can be assembled into narratives of hope and the realization of another outcome. This is beyond Pollyanna, as it deals with the reality of how we encounter difficult experiences and give space with courage to see how another story may be realized. This is the power of Alcoholics Anonymous, whose participants patiently wade through the brokenness of addiction but come out on the other side living a deeper life.

The narrative therapist adds the notion of relentless optimism to this work of exploration. In mining for meaning, the therapist can assume that some larger power is at work in our personal and collective stories to realize God's dream for us. This is a difficult truth for the one who's working their way through a problem-laden story. This generous truth does not gloss over the negative aspects of our stories. Instead, it seeks out the redemptive possibilities in which the storyteller can recognize the larger hand at work in these stories. Optimism is needed in order to recognize the work of this larger hand.

• **Pay attention to the way stories are shaped by rituals.** How did your family observe rituals in their life together prior to your arrival? How did the family mark significant events (holidays, births, deaths, weddings, divorces, family gatherings, ways of identification as a family, etc.)?

Robert Fulghum claims that, from beginning to end, the rituals of our lives shape each hour, day, and year. Everyone leads a ritualized life. Rituals are repeated patterns of meaningful acts. If you are mindful of your actions, you will see the ritual patterns. If you see the patterns, you may understand them. If you understand them, you may enrich them. In this way, the habits of a lifetime become sacred.

He supports his beliefs about rituals with the following propositions: To be human is to be religious. Who am I? What am I doing here? Where did I come from before birth and what happens after I die? What's right and wrong, and how do I know? What is the meaning of life, and how do

I give meaning to my life? How do I account for the awesome, mysterious majesty of the universe, and what's my place in the scheme of things?

To be religious is to be mindful. When careful attention is given to these questions, we find answers and hold to those answers with faith and devotion, thereby making them sacred. The asking and answering process itself sanctifies existence, and we repeat the process throughout our lives. Ritual is the name given to this repetition. Our lives are endless repetition. Fulghum observes the rituals we live in everyday life and notes that

- To be mindful is to pay attention.
- To pay attention is to sanctify existence.

- Rituals are one way in which attention is paid.
- Rituals arise from the stages and ages of life.
- Rituals transform the ordinary into the holy.

- Rituals may be public, private, or secret.
- Rituals may be spontaneous or arranged.
- Rituals are in constant evolution and reformation.

- Rituals create sacred time.
- Sacred time is the dwelling place of the Eternal.
- Haste and ambition are the adversaries of sacred time.[6]

- **Finally, understand the power of liminality.** Liminality is the threshold of whatever change is before you. Liminality is the result of cultural anthropologists who study cultures around the world and explore how persons use ritual to create a map of growth, from one stage to the next, from beginning to end. All across the arc of life, we face liminal moments when we muster the courage to move forward to face whatever is "next" in life. There are small challenges that happen occasionally and often without our noticing them. There are also large liminal moments that give us pause as we contemplate the reality that once we accept the challenge before us, we cannot (and nor do we wish to) go back. There are age-appropriate liminal moments that are observed and noted from many vantage points. These liminal moments are the stuff of life. They are what life is made of and we would do well to notice them and give them the importance they deserve. The narrative process recognizes that people who explore their stories are engaged as active participants in the embrace of liminal moments in order to grow.

The older boundary of adolescence may appear arbitrary depending on the situation the older youth is living. Drawing the line between one stage to the next can be anecdotal according to one's embracing of adult challenges, chiefly accepting the new realities of making one's own decisions and accepting the consequences of those decisions whether successful or not. Adolescence does not merely refer to one's awakening sexuality; it stands for the transitional period from the dependency of childhood to an ever-increasing independence (better, interdependency) of adulthood. It's an in-between stage linking childhood to adulthood.

Different cultures mark this transition differently. How do we in our culture mark these distinctions? Discuss how we describe this in-between state of not a child, not an adult. Victor Turner (mid-twentieth century cultural anthropologist and ethnographer) established research that studied how Central African tribes ritualized the move from childhood to adulthood. He considered this transition "a social drama" that involved tribal rituals and rites known and understood by the tribe as how a child became an adult.

According to the Merriam Webster Dictionary, the term liminal (adj.) means "1. Of, relating to, or situated at a sensory threshold; barely perceptible or capable of eliciting a response liminal visual stimuli, 2. Of, relating to, or being an intermediate state, phase, or condition; in-between, transitional."[7]

Liminality is an ambiguous period of limbo characterized by humility, seclusion, tests, and communitas (an unstructured community where all members are equal). In tribal practice, the boy was taken from the care of the women, where his life as a boy was experienced. The men of the tribe would give the boy to the tribal elders for a period of testing. When that ritual came to an end, he was released to the tribal life of the men and did not reenter the social world of the women. This liminal experience was a time "betwixt and between" when the boy was no longer a part of the society he had been a part of as a boy, yet not reincorporated into that society as a man.

Adolescents fall under the category of liminal beings through their biological and social functions. Puberty and early adolescence are commonly defined as transitional periods between childhood and adulthood. Constant physical changes, for example, make it impossible to root a teenager in a single social status for an extended time. Most teenagers carry the confused burden of having to behave in a more mature, adult fashion (as opposed to acting like a child), yet they are restricted from accessing all of the rights awarded to legal adults; this is commonly referred to as having "all of the responsibility and none of the perks." Hence teenagers are relegated to the liminal state in which they have to somehow configure their own precarious identities. Other young individuals, particularly college and graduate students, who are legally considered adults but still hampered by certain dependencies (such as financial support from parents or lenders, or still enrolled in school instead of having a full-time job), can also claim a liminal identity. Youth are seldom fully independent, even though that's the focus of the shift of power that occurs between parents and youth. Parents are learning to let go and youth are learning how to live responsibly.

Other growth fronts critical to this period are

• **Intellectual.** I am now moving from concrete thinking to thinking in functional, abstract ways. How do I hold two opposing views in balance? How do I use the new tools of critical thinking, empathy, and satire?

• **Moral.** I am now making ethical choices about self, others, and directions in life. How do I know right from wrong and how to handle moral ambiguities?

• **Spiritual.** Who is God? What is a spirituality that works? What about other religions or no religion? What spiritual practice do I want to live?

• **Emotional.** How do I navigate my emotional life that is often both sharply focused and ambiguous (depression, anxiety, narcissism)?

• **Worldview.** I am now aware of social injustice, war, famine, suffering, political power, and abuse. How shall I respond?

Who am I? As I grow on all these fronts, I will also make *big* decisions about who I will be, who I want to travel through life with as friends and lovers, what I will do as a vocation, what my ongoing life of curiosity will embrace, how I will make a mark in life. How will I be happy? Fulfilled? Meaningful?

Know that this is only the beginning of such growth fronts. This is the template of life that they can carry forward. Hopefully adolescents will grow into adulthood open to further growth and become lifelong students of their inner and outer worlds.

Discuss: How did you and your parents navigate this liminal, in-between period? How did it go? Did you do this well, or did you struggle or even fail?

• **Close each session with an honest review.** At the end of each session, ask, "How's this going? What has been meaningful in how our group is functioning? Are there any changes we want to consider to make our experience better?"

Living a Narrative Life

When a writer uses first person and is not writing fiction, it's typically an indicator of either an autobiography or a memoir. This book is anecdotally the latter and certainly not the former. So what is the difference between autobiography and memoir? There are no strict boundaries, but the two forms generally revolve around the difference between "what happened" and "what I think about what happened." A memoir presents what the writer has selected as a version of their story that is told for the purpose of connecting that story's contributions to the arc of life.[8] My purpose in what follows is to see how our stories, yours and mine, while appearing to be random, can be plotted on a graph as telling a larger story that encompasses every stage along the arc of life. Our stories are dots along the arc that runs from beginning to end. We live storied lives, and if we pay attention, we can see how these stories shimmer with meanings that deepen and enrich our experience.

This book is only a memoir in the spirit of asking you, the reader, to use bits and pieces of my story as an enticement to reflect on your own stories. When I tell you my story, the parts that are universal in anyone's story causes you to want to tell me your story. You may become so engaged in the memory of your own story that you interrupt my story to tell me yours. Maybe we should establish the house rules before either of us starts talking.

Naturally, reflecting on our stories spills into other arenas, most of which demonstrate the interconnectedness of life—how all things come from the same place and how we're all connected in some mysterious way. Steve, my teaching partner,[9] has captured a surprising number of his stories by writing them down in his journal. He considers them all self-existent tales, separate and unique, each lightly connected to the others like pearls on a string, a catena of stories that have a beginning, a middle, and an end. By honoring each story as having value, he has written whole notebooks filled with these individual stories covering all seasons of his life. He retrieves them from his memory vault where such experiences are stored and listens to them intently. Then he writes them out in longhand in what Anne Lamott would call "the shitty first draft."[10] Typically, he lets them season for a bit in that form until he returns to them with curious questions that help him tease out more details that he missed in the first draft. He is not polishing the story; he's taking a story first rendered in black and white and colorizing it.

No single telling of a story contains every bit and piece of the story itself. There's always more—more details, more information, more assumptions, more meaning. Narrative psychologists imagine that every story is an edited story, that a certain meaning is derived because the storyteller has either consciously or unconsciously edited the story to suit a purpose. However, in order to edit the story, some story fragments must fall to the editing room floor. Each fragment allows that there are further meanings that have been edited out of the story. With curiosity, one can retrieve these fragments and consider whether a new story, a different story with new meanings, may be derived. With the care of an archaeologist, a person can reintroduce each fragment to see what different understanding may emerge. Memory must be wooed for depth and meaning, and consequently most of us tell thin versions of our stories. Seasoning them as Steve does allows the stories to thicken. Even the slightest additional detail gives a rich patina to our stories. Embedded meaning comes from the thickening process.

Moreover, with first drafts and later iterations that are focused by reflection, Steve goes one step further by giving these stories a headline. A headline is a descriptive handle on how the story works and why it is meaningful, perhaps revealing an insight into its importance. Headlines have a way of finding the heart of the story and announcing it in the simplest terms. They can also be the teaser that draws the listener closer. This level of care and intention gives significance to each story. I believe Steve is a steward of his life who seriously embraces his stories and values them for how they contribute to the depth of his experience. He and I tell our stories to one another freely and find ways to use them purposefully with the groups we lead.

This is the richness of life: to know your own stories, to value and understand them, and to share them with others. In doing so, we are all enriched. By thickening our stories, we thicken our lives. We are stewards of life by owning all of its parts, our successes and our failures, our honest moments and the shadowy sides of us that we can neither explain nor fully understand. We are stewards by owning these parts as utterly ours. We give meaning to them by accepting them completely, not to baptize them in some "Pollyanna" gilding, but to allow that they are ours. We mine them in search of the meaning that gives them power. To do so is an act of supreme courage taken only by those who wish to understand themselves more deeply.

Stories tossed into the well of life do not need to remain lost to us. Perhaps we tossed them there with great intent. Most often, however, we've mindlessly discounted them, blind to how they might have meaning under the curious scrutiny that suggests that any story, perhaps every story, will have great power when one attends to it in a thoughtful way. We are surprised by how much can be embedded in the slightest memory. This is the point where we continue to edit our stories, seeking to ask curious questions in examining them in order to uncover deeper meaning.

In the blazing heat of mid-summer, I flew to Dallas to be with my family to bury my mother's aunt in the cemetery just outside Sherman where my mother's family is buried. We gathered at the funeral home before the service in order to hug and talk in whispered tones. After the chapel service, we got in our cars for the long drive to the tiny Methodist church and surrounding cemetery. Over the years, the area has been swallowed up by the weekend ranches of affluent Dallasites, and now only the old-timers know it as Cottage Hill.

My mother's family is buried in the northwest corner of the cemetery that surrounds the small white Methodist chapel, and so we had to walk about fifty yards across and through the other family plots to get to the spot readied for my aunt. Everyone walked in silence, partly out of respect for my aunt and partly because of the oppressive heat.

For some reason, this day was different than all the others I had shared with my family. I remembered past times of being out there as a boy and hearing my grandmother tell me never to walk on top of a grave because that was dishonoring to the dead person. So we always walked in ninety-degree turns around the graves at the cemetery, turns that were similar to the roads that took us out there, all with sharp angles around the fields of country farms.

But today, walking among those graves meant something new to me. I looked around and felt surrounded by the long-gone members of my family. I recognized their names etched in stone and could call forth memories of people who had played their part in giving me my boyhood: memories of Christmases past and Thanksgiving dinners that would last for hours, memories of summer evenings playing in the backyard while the adults sat in metal lawn chairs talking and smoking cigarettes and drinking sweet tea.

Standing there in the hot Texas sun for the funeral of my mother's aunt, listening to the minister read a handful of Bible verses, gave me a feeling of warmth derived from my place in this family that I had not previously recognized, even though I had been to Cottage Hill many times before. I could look around at the headstones and sense my own history in the names and dates of those who had gone before, and for the first time I knew who I was. *This family* was *my family*. I was someone connected to these others so deeply that, in growing up, I hardly recognized my place in the family. My identity was hiding in plain sight, and I lacked the understanding to perceive it. My story was connected to all their stories. In fact, my story was an extension of their stories, as if we were all a part of a larger story. Most of this I sensed only in the stories upstream from my own, with little anticipation that the stream flows ever onward toward a future that cannot be recognized until it inhabits the present moment. Nevertheless, the sense of securing one's identity from perceiving the existence of the whole family is a good beginning point.

For me, that experience was a profound moment of adulthood. It was one of those moments that I would not have understood as a young man because I had not lived enough of life yet. I had only experienced life from the perspective of youth and had not fully completed my journey to adulthood. In that moment in the cemetery, I made a turn in life that I want to use to help shape our thoughts. Sitting among the silent, stone symbols of my family's history and heritage, I finally understood enough of my past to realize that my identity as a person flowed out of the people who had gone before me.

One of the developmental goals as we grow into adults is to be able to embrace an individuated personal identity. It's my opinion that our identity is birthed as we are given physical bodies, and this identity grows in the same way our bodies do. For a good while, we move through childhood and adolescence under an assumed identity, a borrowed identity if you will, living under the shelter of our parents and deflecting the need to hammer out a separated identity until the time when we are forced to face the issue directly. Some of us move through that stage without much trauma, and some of us struggle every step of the way and resist at every turn. We may even struggle in contradiction to the identity shelter our family has provided, especially if it is unstable or dysfunctional—although plenty of young people from supportive homes struggle this way.

There is nothing simple about this work of self. This is the inner struggle we must engage at one point or the other. It seems most are challenged by something that exerts enough stress on our inner world to cause us to grow and change. It may be so pointed as to be a dramatic conversion when we refuse to live in the old world and become travelers in a new world equipped with a new clarity about who we are and who we are not.

In one of Gabriel García Márquez's fables, he tells of a tribe stricken with a devastating plague of insomnia.[11] The sleeplessness leads to such forgetfulness that the members of the tribe even forget what some things are named. They fight the plague by writing down the names of things they need to remember. The amnesia becomes so bad, however, that they eventually forget how to read. The decline from sleeplessness to forgetfulness to illiteracy is what we now suffer in our culture: we not only do not know; we also do not know that we do not know.

This is a good illustration of what it means to struggle with identity. We do not know, or at least we have forgotten, who we are. Our forgetfulness about our past becomes a piece of the puzzle of our identity that we have forgotten or discarded, and we limp along until we either realize our forgetfulness or give up. When we give up, the memories tied to our identity are lost altogether.

There is a narrative process we can adopt that helps us peel away the layers of our stories. We can ask questions that help open up our story rather than stating declarations that close it down. Typically, the stories we know from childhood are assigned to us by our family elders in a prescribed, stilted form. The meanings we've attached to many of our childhood stories are given to us by others. We've been told these stories so often that they become a part of the family lore, and these edited stories may need examination in adulthood to challenge their meaning and to add a new understanding to what the story is really about. Unpacking the stories that have been foisted upon us may lead us to an "aha" moment of new insight, but what the stories mean may only be defined by the way others describe them. Maybe we are the object of shame and ridicule in such stories, and we have never challenged or questioned those assignations. Perhaps the story is told at our expense and for the entertainment of others. As curious adults, with great courage, we can return to these well-trod stories and explore them for other meanings and other outcomes until, ultimately, they help us know ourselves better. The people who have defined these stories for us may resist when we try to revisit them. In spite of that, we must have the courage to explore them and a willingness to go deeper than the simple veneer others have laid over them.

There is a cumulative power in the whole of these stories, a vein that can be mined, deepening our sense of self with new mercy, forgiveness, and tolerance that may have been missed before. In deepening these old stories, we locate the three-dimensional characters that inhabit them rather than the thin versions we have always heard about. We may even discover that these stories are not about us but are instead about others who perpetuate them. When we revisit what we thought we knew, we can distance ourselves from the tales that used to define us or, worse, shackle us to an outdated version of who we really are. I have welcomed the companionship of my brothers and my cousin (more of a sister-cousin since we were cared for by our maternal grandmother five days a week) as we revisit old stories from childhood; each of us gets to hear a once-familiar story through someone else's perspective. They have their own versions of the same events I'm recalling for myself.

Stories have the power to draw us together, and thus they are made for community. A community can be two people, but it becomes even stronger when others are added. My wish in writing this book is that we break open new meaning in life by exploring our stories in a community where we feel safe and where our presence is part of an interconnected circle of friends.

We frame our lives by recalling our experiences in story form. It's how we make sense of both the past and the present. Can stories also predict the future? We seldom have such clarity as to see how the past will create suggestions about the future, but a deeper understanding of the "upstream" stories of our past can shine a light on the possibilities of stories that are "downstream." The old saw is that "we become more and more of what we already are." The details will remain fuzzy, but the patterns will emerge and that alone can give us guidance.

Stories are the repository of life's experiences that enables us to know who we are. In contrast to our dreams, they are filtered to tell the story we want them to tell. We shape our stories for purpose and empower them with meanings that may or may not have been a part of the actual experience. These tales are often the way we judge ourselves, casting hidden and necessary meanings upon our self-understanding. Collectively, our stories and how we tell them map life as we understand it. Each story can be dissected as a unique moment, but when we string them together they add up to the telling of who we are, why we exist, what we think or believe, and what might happen next.

Story is a way of seeing, a way of organizing experience, and a way of making sense of life. Novelist Morris West, in *The Clowns of God*, wrote, ". . . man [*sic*] is a creature who walks in two worlds and traces upon the walls of his cave the wonders and the nightmare experiences of his spiritual pilgrimage."[12] We are all painting stories on our cave walls. We are exploring our own experiences by making stories out of them and reflecting on their meaning. Once you tell one story, you'll tell a million of them. Once you frame a single event in story form, every significant life event will fall into that form, and you will recognize them as the hidden jewels they are and will want to begin collecting them.

All of life is a story. These essays are written in order to help us use certain frameworks to explore our lives. They offer a way to think about life through lived experiences that are loosely labeled "narrative." There are narrative storytellers who may call themselves comedians or cultural commentators, or who may be the focal point of a gang of listeners who want to hear a good tale told with passion and humor. There are narrative preachers who elevate the sacred stories from their prosaic settings and breathe life into them so that current listeners can feel as though they inhabit those old stories. There are narrative therapists who help patients listen to their own stories and give them courage in exploring those stories for insight and growth. There are narrative structures derived from the notion that all of life is a story. But there's more; these essays are also built on a platform of an existential understanding of all these stories. We are a meaning-making people who experience the pendulum of life lived between experience and reflection. Things happen and we ponder their meaning. When significant events occur, we go deep, seeking to know why those events have such power for us.

There is a wish to understand how a larger hand is at work in our stories. One does not need to be a faith practitioner or a member of a certain religion to sense this larger hand. In this book, I've written about religious experience in the model of the Unitarian-Universalists or the nonsectarian. In that light, one's belief is one's own, but it is not imposed upon anyone else. Neither is it presented as a form of ultimate truth. This respects others and allows them some breathing room. In a narrative community, people support and challenge each other and also create ample room for integrity, curiosity, meaning, and purpose.[13]

How do we interpret the unplanned events that shape and redirect our lives? Outside the protection of our home of origin, we begin to experience life most directly, with all its highlights and lowlights. Some events seem to give direction to where we're headed and how we will get there. Most younger adults are not skilled at life planning just yet, but they are beginning to understand that planning is necessary for getting where they want to go. Willy-nilly is not a pathway to success.

How can one make sense of the senseless things that happen? How can one understand events that pop up unexpectedly and alter the trajectory of life? Making sense is the issue, but where are the tools we can use to make sense of things? What happens when the normal course of life is altered? What do we do with the interruption that takes over our life's story?

It can be the simplest of things, the intrusion that no one can see coming. No matter what the cause, when life's direction is broken, the whole of life takes a new turn. James Loder, professor of pastoral theology at Princeton known for his research about convictional moments (any event that forces an inner change in outlook or commitment), described unexpected life events as "transforming moments."[14] As he was assisting a woman with a flat tire at dusk on a busy highway, a trucker who was falling asleep at the wheel plowed through the woman's car and also Loder's own car and trailer that were parked just ahead. The woman's car rolled over Loder, crushing and injuring him severely. Loder says that, as he lingered between life and death, he experienced a mystical encounter with the divine that would mark his life from that point forward. This event became a transforming moment that altered his outlook, making him willing to follow the mysterious promptings of the "slender threads" and leading him down paths he would otherwise never have followed in both his academic life and his inner world of perceiving. ("Slender threads," as explained by Robert Johnson, are any unplanned gift or curse of circumstance that alters the trajectory of our lives. They are the counter melody to our wish to intentionally direct our path through the decisions we make. They are the steps we take as a means of controlling our future. The slender threads are happenstances we don't control but that control us.[15])

I imagine a two-part model that swings like a pendulum between event and reflection. Loder's model expands my simplistic notion of the pendulum movement, widening the conversation to a five-stage logic of the human spirit: conflict, scanning, insight, release, and interpretation/

verification. So deep was Loder's transformation after this incident that he faced a change in the contours of human existence, now believing that it included the four dimensions of the self, the world, the Void, and the Holy. His inner experience of reality was radically altered by this violent intrusion into his old world. Loder's professional academic world had focused on the border separating psychotherapy and traditional Reformed theology, but now he found himself seeking meaning about an event that disrupted how he experienced both realms of knowledge. It allowed him to break through to a transformed way of knowing. These kinds of deeply experienced events have the power to transform us from a shallow understanding to a depth of knowing that may be difficult to describe to others who have not experienced such events.

Some talk knowingly about what they call "God's will." Most talk beyond what they know or at least with a noticeable lack of humility about such conversations. Much of this kind of talk is a less-than-veiled version of determinism that depicts God as the director of the drama who controls small and large events in our lives. How else do we make sense of the flow of events? The argument made by determinism has a limited appeal because it is based on a world in which circumstances must be hung on God's whim. Surely those who insist on "God's will" allow some kind of provisional explanation for mysterious events or occurrences they do not like and cannot explain. Is there no room for mystery in assigning blame or credit to God?

Have you ever found yourself carried on the capricious winds of circumstance? Have you ever felt as though your life were guided by a whimsical feather blowing in the warm wind, carried aloft above the tree-tops so that you might land who knows where? Maybe it's as simple as being in the right (or wrong) place at the right (or wrong) time, or meeting someone who steers you in a new but unpredictable direction. It could be as simple as an unexpected good fortune (maybe you hit the lottery with your pool at work), or it could be an accident or tragedy. In those moments of redirection, we might be tempted to move on without reflecting. Nevertheless, we are meaning-making persons who either accept the challenge of reflection or who demonstrate little curiosity about why things have happened or understanding about what those events might mean to us.

Often our lives are given direction by the mystery of the slender threads that occur. Even though we think our willful determination guides our lives, life has another wisdom, and we are somehow inspired, guided, or managed (even mismanaged) by unseen forces outside our control. Even though we exert our free will and make plans and set goals and proceed with full confidence as if we are in control, it also seems true that there is a larger hand at work in directing us through life. Call it fate or blind luck, call it destiny, or call it the hand of God. Call it what you will, but know that there are events and plans we control, and there are intrusions and surprises we don't control.

I often use the phrase "as fate would have it" as a robust way of observing that we twist and turn on the events that occur in our lives; sometimes they are good events and sometimes they are tragic. But on occasion, more often than we can know, even the tragic events tend to act positively in our regard. Sometimes we make the smallest, most imperceptible turn and our lives are spared. Sometimes our lives fall into the deepest despair. A job is offered or a job is taken away. We get a phone call and with it our lives are changed. Inexplicably, we take a turn here or a twist there, and the arc of our lives unpredictably shifts and twists in a new direction.

Barbara Brown Taylor tells us that providence "is not about God's will overriding our own. It is more like a dance, that totally mysterious dance that takes place between God's freedom and our freedom, between God's will and our own."[16] Are fate and whimsy merely the shallow end of the pool where we cannot see how God is involved in our lives? God's job is not to prevent bad things from happening or to make good things happen. God is not tipping the scales in anyone's direction, nor is God putting a hedge of protection around us so we are not harmed. Simple observation seems to justify these arguments. God's job is to stay present in our lives, creating whole worlds out of total chaos, breathing life into piles of dust, making something new out of the unfathomable wreckage of our lives. Maybe that's not miracle enough for some, but for others it's an open-hearted and generous argument for the miraculous.

The opening line of Robert Johnson's memoir names a pivotal life event that put him on a path of lifelong reflection: "It all began with the crash of a car against the brick wall and the small knee of an eleven-year-old boy caught in between." Johnson sees the imprint of this event writ large across every day beyond that one day. He sees the shadow of his wounding across the arc of his life and knows that every common experience of existence was marked forever by this singular event. How are we to see God's hand in such a moment? We are only given a vague notion of how or why the car crashed on the sidewalk, trapping the young boy's leg and scarring him for life. The way Johnson tells this story, he sees beyond cause and looks to meaning as he interprets the event as a life-altering moment. Johnson is clear in his long assessment of this event's occurrence—both the randomness and the specificity of its effects. He can see that he was forced to mine the meaning out of this event with intent, by widening his view of life to allow that what happened did indeed bring about changes in him that he could not identify until he was able to unravel the layers of meaning.[17]

Life-altering events may occur in any stage of life: childhood, adolescence, or at any point in adulthood. Some people go through such moments in their twenties or at midlife. While there's less time on the clock as one navigates older adulthood, the result of such a pivotal event is the same. Life ambles along in a generally planned or lived direction, what some would call "normal time," until something unexpected occurs and life takes an immediate and unplanned new direction. Most of us cannot anticipate this occurrence; we have no idea that something dramatically different is about to occur. The list of how these events might happen is endless.

Forrest Church defines religion as "our human response to the dual reality of being alive and knowing we must die," meaning we make meaning of our existence on the one hand and our death on the other hand.[18] Between those two truths, the whole of life's arc is lived. Between the two is the ground upon which faith is based. These two large ideas lead some to make a religious commitment that somehow makes sense of life. Others, however, use their own sensibilities to determine that no faith is needed and make meaning out of the arc of life on its own merits. How and why we answer the question of meaning indicates how we use the resources of our faith to make meaning when meaningful events occur. In the narrative exploration, whether or not one is religious, we are engaged in using the resources of faith to answer the big questions.

These unexpected events can occur when we're the only ones involved, or they can ensnare others who are drawn into the same drama. They can be adverse events, but, on occasion, they are so filled with joy as to be serendipitous. What crosses our paths are typically run-of-the-mill events. Most are speed bumps and a few are earth-shattering. We may choose to interpret these events with a religious curiosity. One may or may not use faith to supply the answer to the question of why. For many, this the question of Job and the question of religious philosophers across the ages. "Why do bad things happen to good people?" This is ancient business and we seem to have few resources within us to deal with our questions. For many, faith in a larger being is a beginning point that may lead us in ever-widening circles of meaning. The key interpretive clues are there, but they demand that we embrace them with an open mind, an open heart, and brutal honesty.

It's my firm belief that we can view our stories as sources of self-understanding and draw from them for guidance in our search for meaning. Each of them has something to offer in our search. Each can bring a bit of clarity. Platitudes seem disconnected from the demands of life. Moralizing is no more than a form of behavioral emptiness, a parental wish to control people rather than enrich them through self-understanding. The narrative challenge is to find meaning in those events that seem counter to our understanding. This process of narrative thought gives us the tools to steer away from platitudes so we might be present with the one who is struggling. We can find new meaning in the event itself that allows one another to seek depth rather than dismiss someone's pain because we can't bear to join them in their struggle.

We will observe two guiding principles in this book. The first is that life is lived on an arc of time and experience, and almost everyone follows this arc as a universal map of experience. Our earliest stories show that the ancients recognized this map, but only in the last century or so have the stages of life been understood so clearly. Sigmund Freud and Carl Jung both elaborated on these important developmental markers, but Erik Erikson laid out the detailed stages by which we understand "the arc of life." Almost everyone who writes in the field of life development uses Erikson's work as a reference point. Psychologists in the post-Erikson era have taken his structures as the most complete framework available. Others have built on, amended, and revised it to settle on frameworks that are more useful for understanding the human experience across the arc of life.

The most useful adaptation in my estimation has been Donald Capps's *The Decades of Life*, a work that makes sense of life by seeing it as a decadal pathway.[19] This significant reframing comes at the beginning of the arc, the series of infant stages heavily weighted by Freud's initial emphasis on the oral, anal, and genital stages. While not discounting these psychodynamic stages, Capps sees the first decade as a whole part instead of a series of intra-psychic stages. Then he uses the decadal model to describe what happens in adolescence and the stages of adulthood. While the Freudian model is minimized, Capps is able to give a strong decadal understanding to the adult stages. For the non-psychologically trained layperson, this model makes more sense in the stages that matter most than it might in the intensive focus on infant, toddler, and preschool needs. This book will follow Capps's model to help interpret life stages; admittedly I am simplifying both Capps's and Erikson's models to guide the reader through a less restricted approach that will allow us to focus on the value of the stories themselves. I encourage you to consider stories with soft boundaries from one stage to the other.

The second guiding principle is the fact that rituals play a strong role in the nature of narrative work. Rituals are a way to hold up certain truths and declare them as significant. They are representative ways in which we embed certain activities with great meaning. Poet and essayist Thomas Lynch says about rituals, "We act out things we cannot put in words."[20] When we observe closely the series of stories that surface in narrative activities, we can see the shaping presence of rituals and how they are woven into our lives, even when we're not aware of them. They are crucial to seeking deeper meanings. In rituals, we are acting out stories that have been scripted before our time, and we find our stories evident in the stories of others who have made their own journeys before us. Narratives are always closely aligned with rituals; they are often embedded with common symbolic behaviors that reenact highly meaningful universal stories. Our stories are frequently created in the workshop of acting out rituals that help us make meaning in particular stories we are experiencing. Rituals are "essential for our survival by establishing courtship, organizing the hunt, caring for offspring, and avoiding life-threatening conflicts"—basic goals of a human life.[21] To be clear, Anderson and Foley are describing our psychological, social, and religious survival more than our biological survival. For them, rituals are more about our *being*, perhaps our well-being, beyond our mere existence.

Rituals are the means by which the world works. They make the world habitable and worth living. They are the vehicles for finding meaning in life's experiences. And this is where rituals connect to narratives: both are means for achieving the same ends. One might consider how each of them, stories and rituals, are a part of our core sense of self. Erik Erikson reminds us that rituals enable us to enter into relationships and make significant connections with others and the world. We enter life in observed rituals, and, in great and small ways, those rituals help us know ourselves. They are the windows through which the breezes of self are understood. Children insist that bedtime rituals be observed with unbending exactitude. Preschoolers act out domestic chores or replay their favorite TV shows, complete with costumes and the recruitment of younger ones to fulfill whatever roles are demanded of them. Sibling strife can erupt whenever the recruits act on their own and don't follow the script. No matter the stage of life, we all live according to the scripts of rituals. Anderson and Foley contend that narratives and rituals are distinct but not separate. They have much in common, but they are not two sides of the same coin. Perhaps they have a kind of symbiotic relationship where each needs the other in order to exist or to sow the seedlings of life.

Less scholarly and more anecdotal, Robert Fulghum's book *From Beginning to End: The Rituals of Our Lives* is poignant and enlightening. Fulghum writes about "the big moments" when we gather for rituals. But he is also deeply aware of all the small moments when we are engaged in ritual behavior and give no thought to how those activities structure our lives. He makes his case for clear-eyed observations about the mundane with a guiding list of propositions. Fulghum is an open-hearted nonsectarian, and yet he claims the obvious, that "to be human is to be religious. To be religious is to be mindful. To be mindful is to pay attention. To pay attention is to sanctify existence."[22]

Sometimes rituals are disconnected from the stories that brought them into being. In those cases, the rituals are practiced but they are without meaning and will not keep the story alive from one generation to the next. Most of life is built on the foundation of observing rituals. We make every stage of life a ritual that we celebrate and observe. Likely the movement across the arc of life, from one stage to the next, will come with corresponding rituals by which we recognize that we are indeed changing stages. Your birth is recognized throughout your entire life as a birthday, a ritual observance designed to remember the day you took your place in life. Your birthday has likely been remembered and celebrated by family and friends. One of the best-loved features of being on Facebook or other forms of social media is hearing from "friends"—people with whom we usually have no contact except that they are part of our social media community—and so birthday wishes come from all points on the globe: from extended family, from high school or college friends, and from the bevy of people we've met through work or social groups. Your birthday will take on added significance when you hit the big markers, usually an age that ends with "0," as in the decadal model. Other significant mile markers could be age 21, when Americans can legally buy alcoholic drinks; age 33, the "Jesus year" (he is thought to have died on the cross at that age); age 55, known as "double nickels"; or age 65, the age of Medicare. No matter what decade we're in, our rituals help us understand how to feel about coming to such ages.

We ritualize every liminal moment: first tooth, first steps, first tooth lost, potty-training and getting out of diapers, picking out and putting on our own clothes. Almost every "first" is ritualized. But this doesn't stop in childhood. We continue to make rituals around the deaths of beloved pets or the loss of beloved grandparents. We make rituals about the first day of school, passing our driving test, and high school graduation. First date, first kiss, first time to make love—all are meaningful stages of our interpersonal lives that are observed for the power they engender about life's great mysteries. The list of ritualized stages of life is nearly endless, but the rituals have a life-giving quality for how we understand and explore stories.

Our understanding of rituals was first described by anthropologists who studied a variety of cultures and noted the power and meaning of rituals as unique windows into societal structures. They looked at rites of passage in those societies, especially those unique but intense passages when a child becomes an adult. The individual and the larger society are guided into recognizing that the individual has successfully moved from one stage of growth and now inhabits the next stage. At the heart of ritual is the action that demonstrates the change in a way that words cannot.

We have other stories not based on rituals, but we certainly can see how rituals and the ways we observe them are powerful embodiments of our lives upon the greater arc. Rituals act like mile markers on our maps. We link memory to the rituals we develop around significant milestones. Our vault of memories are not limited to these ritualized observances, but the rituals do form the mainframe of our memories, giving structure to the whole arc of life from beginning to end.

Fulghum's propositions are intentionally inclusive; he casts a wide net in which all people can think more deeply about the insignificant habits of being so that we can see patterns, both unique and universal, that help us embrace our humanity. Ritual, in Fulghum's understanding, involves repeated, patterned, personal expressions of our internal structure of self and security. Many of these patterns have been ingrained, obtained from others who helped in our formation—people who may have unconsciously passed along the habits of being that they received in a similar way from someone else. Such is the nature of many of our rituals. Once we recognize the patterns of everyday rituals, we will see them everywhere. These practices will enlighten us to our own behavior and may even give us a reason to chuckle at ourselves. They also help us (1) to recognize more clearly the larger, communal acts of ritual that help us know who we are and (2) to embrace important thresholds as we move from one stage of life to the next.

In the end, this book is an invitation to explore your stories. Look over the library of events and people that tell your story. Everyone has a life story composed of hundreds, perhaps thousands, of stories, but few hold them closely enough to scrutinize what they are about. Novelist Frederick

Buechner phrases the invitation this way: "Listen to your life. All moments are key moments."[23]

Listen to your life. Take in the extraordinary commonness of all your stories—not in the hopes of inflating the stories into memories that did not happen but in order to draw closer to them, plunge their depths, and deepen the meaning of what you have experienced. Buechner's invitation is extended to all who are curious enough to explore the key moments. He writes, ". . . it seems to me that no matter who you are, and no matter how eloquent or otherwise, if you tell your story with sufficient candor and concreteness, it will be an interesting story and in some sense a universal story."[24]

We have one another as fellow travelers on the same paths together. Why don't we tell one another our stories?

The Emergence of the Self

I am the one behind the eyeballs. I am the one behind the cranium's facial structure with its latitude and longitude. I am the one behind the face's scars and lines, behind the skull's circumference and spatial relationships, behind the slightly irregular nose squarely between the eyes and mouth and chin and matching ears. I am the one behind the wordless warmth of a welcoming smile, behind the understated cynicism of a well-placed smirk, behind the downturned lips that undergird the fierce glare of the eyes. With this body, I need no words to communicate whole worlds of meanings. I am a walking billboard of meaning with this body of mine.

I am the one who lives inside this body and its angular dimensions of height and weight and length, this body with its metrics that define the uniqueness of my physical being. In the beginning not quite able to separate me from you, not seeing me for my individuality or you for your importance to me by being separate and unique, I am caught in the web of coexistence and forced to walk the fine line between independence and dependence. There's the polarity between the personal and the non-personal, between dependence and independence, but in between, there's the verdant middle ground because of the interdependence we have with others.

I am the one with this skin pigmentation, its texture and hues, color-coordinated with hair and iris. I am male or female but not limited in the rich variety of inhabiting my gender with all its polarities, needs, and expressions. I am embodied in the world. My body and all its complexities have shaped my inner being, but no doubt my inner self has given meaning to this body I inhabit. From the beginning I lived in total unity, self and body, until I learned I could live more acutely in one realm or the other, but never in isolation from either. The gift of consciousness is the gift of thought and self-awareness, with words and phrases and half-thoughts to describe the world I inhabit with my body and my mind.

How shall I describe the connection between the me within and my body without? My body is more than just a container in which I reside. I am grounded in human flesh, and as it goes in one, so it goes in the other as body and self are mysteriously, inexplicably connected. We cannot separate the two; we can only explore the intertwining of one with the other. How do I learn to make sense of this mystery? I am mortal flesh, with a body susceptible to weakness, stress, disease, and the amazing capacity to live in some symbiotic relationship to my inner world.

No matter, I am the one who awakened to consciousness within this body. I was a watcher of the world I could see until I realized I was more than a body, became aware that I had thoughts, language both tender and powerful, wordless emotions I was coming to express. Consciousness understood in sensate triggers helped me differentiate hunger, pain, pleasure, and release. I also understood through the receptors of my body when I was warm or cold, exhausted and in need of sleep, or soothed and comforted. All of these are extensions of the me living inside this corpus of creation.

With no thought of need or choice, I am a dreamer with the gift of consciousness that extends beyond wakefulness into the sleeping life of a mind that never rests. Having little need for structured thought or order, my dreams run through the blender, wild and ever changing. My dreams have no boundaries, unafraid to risk the drama of the unimaginable because it is in my dreams that everything, every thought, every action, every emotion can and will be expressed.

I am a thinker but I am not quiet, holding conversations with myself whether I'm listening or not. I am a thinking person with an inner thought life that is never silent. If there's not a focused topic of interest, something to fixate on, I will create a sufficient level of conflicting noises to fill the inner void. The chatter of my thoughts is mostly uncensored and unbending in brutal honesty. Sometimes my commentary is formed by words, phrases, and occasionally in complete sentences as though I am talking with someone. People talk to themselves all the time. Most know they do this, but some don't seem to notice. All they've done is embarrass themselves by giving their kooky inner thoughts a voice. But if they don't mind, is it embarrassment or self-slander? Other times my thinking is composed of no words, no specificity, as if I'm not focused, conscious but not aware of my own thoughts, more like images with no words as no words are needed. These are the images for which words were created as symbols of realities that need no formed language.

Even so, it was the gift of language that widened the world to me. With language, I can reflect upon my life; I can use language to describe my inner world and speak with those in my outer world. Language is my portal to worlds I encounter in either my lived or imagined experience. The power of naming things is the particular gift of representational language that paints the world in hues and shapes. I have this language and yet I know my language is a part of the cacophony of human voices scatter-cast by a broad hand around the world. My own language is propped up by stolen words and ideas from other word families. We are beggars and thieves whenever we hear a glittering word or are captivated by a shiny phrase, adopting it to brighten our own dull language.

But what about that time before I had language? What about those days when I had thoughts but no words? Is language what consciousness has to have in order to exist? Is language the requisite tool needed to get along in life? Are words and their meanings the end result or merely the tools for consciousness? How did I describe my view of the world before words? What is thought stripped away from the language used to map and measure experience?

❧

All of us live under the influence of an inner world where everything (every sensate experience, every emotion, every thought) is stored. Our inner world contains a storehouse of memory where everything is remembered, whether it's consciously available to us or not. Nothing is tossed aside or thrown away. Gabriel García Márquez wrote, "Life is not what one lived, but what one remembers and how one remembers it in order to recount it."[25] It's all held fast except for those whose memories have been locked away forever, buried so deep that they resist recall. It's true except when it isn't.

Memories are created when the brain unconsciously edits each lived experience, choosing what to hold for the moment and what to hold for the long term, for *every moment* in our waking life. The content for each moment or experience is overwhelming: visual details, sounds, smells, touch, words, feelings, and significance. Each bit of information is stored in separate parts of the brain and pulled together to construct a representation of the event. It is the hippocampus (the region of the brain entrusted with coordinating the storage of long-term memories) that reunites those bits of information during recall and makes sense of it. The brain even "tags" this information so that another different experience can recall that singular event and bring it alongside the new experience as a moment of recall or déjà vu. Consequently, Daniel Schacter asserts that the brain reconstructs our memories each time we recall them, and he calls that complicated process "re-membering."[26] Each re-membering is unique, as we never recall the memory in the same way twice. Our memories are subject to re-editing, so the memory's meaning and details can be untrustworthy.

Memory researchers estimate that there are 100 billion neurons in the average human brain. Each neuron is capable of handling dozens of connections with other neurons, so you can see the endless possibilities of the universe that exists between the ears. David Hogue explores these possibilities in his book, *Remembering the Future, Imagining the Past: Story, Ritual, and the Human Brain,* in which he describes multiple ways the brain handles information and experiences, both of which are needed for memory to be functional.[27]

The brain operates on two mainframes, *working memory* and *long-term memory.* Working memory is utilitarian, helping us receive information in order to perceive what is happening and then moving us to decision-making and even action. We are constantly assessing what happens around us, ready to make decisions in response. Perhaps a simple example of working memory would be the commute to work, a utilitarian task of how to get from home to work. Most folks adopt a "best route" that is preferred among the endless options they may take according to mood or the challenge of road construction, weather, or traffic hazards. The brain remembers a vast array of options of how to accomplish a task that can be either mindless or subject to the ongoing scrutiny of anxiety and anger.

Long-term memory involves the storage of information for longer than the present moment and bears with it the value of relationships or their meaning. The brain receives from the working memory information that it may judge suitable for retention, for storage as long-term memory. Both levels of memory deal with uncountable bits of information that are capable of being considered in each moment of time. To be sure, working memory and long-term memory are in constant dialogue about the incessant information that's received.

Hogue advances beyond the working and long-term memory, as the brain also controls other dimensions of memory.[28] *Semantic memory* holds a wide-ranging amount of information related to concepts and facts, generic information about the world that enables you to be effective in trivia games. *Procedural memory* holds the skills needed for certain tasks or even habits, likely those that are repetitive in nature. Much of what we do is sequential, demanding that we do certain tasks in a particular order nearly mindlessly. These are meaningful collections of information that are needed for certain tasks or even for certain habitual experiences. Last, there is *autobiographical memory*, which is meaningful to our narrative exploration. In narrative therapy, one psychologist calls this "episodic memory" that provides the recall of events, one after another, either in meaningful sequences or in isolated, singular moments.[29] These episodes are how memory retains experiences free-standing memories or as stories understood as part of a larger whole.

How are memories involved in shaping one's self? Most narrative theorists contend that the self is a constructed identity we create for ourselves through the melding of the sum of life's experiences. There is a core to our personalities that we narrate to others. Richard Hester claims that we create a self-story, a narrative constructed around an understanding of self.[30] In narrative thought, the idea of the self is held in story form, a story told to others so that they tell our stories when they describe us.

William Lowell Randall envisions four different perspectives on the self as a story. These varying perspectives are interwoven elements of a unified narrative about self:

• **Existence**, or the outside story, is the uninterpreted totality of everything I have ever thought, done, said, felt; every minute detail of every millisecond I have lived—thus, the totality of my life. This is a compilation of the whole with no added meaning or interpretation attached.

• **Experience**, or the inside story, is the selection and construction of my existence into a narrative. More specifically, it's what *I* make of the outside story. This perspective holds together my past, my present, and my future. Mostly, it's a story about me that is untellable, even though I give great energy to making sense of it.

• **Expression**, or the inside-out story, is the story I tell others. I have multiple stories in my arsenal of self that I tell when I judge them appropriate. These are often different facets of the same self, and they may be truthful or generously polished versions. I choose which of these facets to share with others to allow them to understand at least one story of me, the one I choose to share.

• **Impression**, or the outside-in story, is the story read into my life by others who know me or encounter me. Again, the stories will vary by those on the outside, depending on the context in which we are connected. I may feel that they "get me" or that these stories prove they don't know me at all. I may or may not have access to these impressions, as they reside in others apart from my knowing.[31]

Nevertheless, our minds create memory from our experience and also go so far as to *construct* those memories into narratives we use to justify our self-stories. Thus, our brains weave these memories into a plot to drive the self-story forward. Our brains naturally work on these episodic memories to construct a life story from the library of memories we have collected. Often, narrative therapists refer to this process as a social construction view of reality. Reality is not observed or discovered; rather, it is constructed in social relationships in which we carefully construct an identity developed through the nature of our interpersonal relationships.

In the last days of the Civil War, in Columbia, South Carolina, Mary Chesnut's diary of March 1865 included this entry: "[Union general] Sherman marched off in solid column, leaving not so much as a blade of grass behind. A howling wilderness, land laid waste, dust and ashes." Her despairing comments record the devastation to the Old South, whose glory had been built upon the old plantation system where African slaves tended massive acres of economically viable crops, thus creating immense wealth for their masters. Mary Chesnut's is one story, but there's another, equally important story that should be told and appreciated as a vital part of the history: while Sherman had destroyed the plantations, the slaves were dancing in the streets.[32]

According to narrative theorists Michael White and David Epston, the brain is engaged in "a selective process in which we prune, from our experience, those events that do not fit with the dominant evolving stories that we and others have about us."[33] Consequently, the stock of our self-stories is limited in scope. There are countless stories that are not included. These stories can be reclaimed in the work of narrative therapy as providing material for refreshed stories through a re-authoring process. *Re-authoring* is the term given to the process of "deepening" our stories.[34] No one story is the whole story. A narrative view of life opens up a deeper world of meanings that emerge as we become adept at narrative practices. Studies in narrative psychology help us understand that our stories are constructed based on an unexplored sense of self. We make sense of what we have to work with, but it's important to realize that even the simplest stories have depth of meaning and that the more one knows of self, these other meanings can emerge. This is the narrative challenge. *Curious questions* are often the means to thinking deeper, and the one who prompts this thinking with an exploratory question invites the storyteller to recognize the other narratives that open up one's story rather than constricting it with worn-out plots that have no new light shed upon them.

As a child crosses over into young adulthood, parents or other elder family members may move from telling the well-worn stories of childhood to helping the young adult understand what that story was about. In my own family, I was in middle adulthood before I knew that my father had been briefly married to someone none of us knew about. My brothers and I didn't understand why we knew so few details about this part of our dad's life. Why the secret? What meaning did it have for my father? What meaning did it have for our mother, who never in my hearing said a word about it? What brought my father and his first wife together, and what prompted them to divorce shortly thereafter and go their own ways? How long were they married? What was our father's first wife's name? What was she like? And so on and so on . . . . The questions are now held by the three of us sons, and we have no answers to give us new light on our own lives.

One can wonder where the ever-judgmental self-critic came from. We draw our lines of self-understanding from voices and experiences outside of ourselves, and we import them into our inner thoughts. We take the judgments of others more seriously than our own judgments. We listen to disreputable sources and allow them to shape our self-images. How else do we explain how truly hard we are on ourselves—in ways that we would never project upon others? We are often our worst critics, and we get our data from suspect, unreliable sources. How long have we carried around these negative images of ourselves that are in complete contrast to how others see us?

Without words to map thought, is there no basis for memory, or are sensory experiences sufficient? Does language create orderliness for sorting experience? Thought that is orderly and parsed out in structured phrases and paragraphs gives us a format for holding things beyond the moment itself. Paul Hoover observes, "we drag expensive ghosts through memory's unmade bed";[35] this is his way of describing everything within us that continues to haunt or bless us, guide or direct us to the place in us where the past, present, and future collide and, on occasion, peaceably coexist.

The mind is constantly busy in either conscious or unconscious thought, and when that's not vivid enough, the self makes its own theater of dream images in our sleep. The show opens every night as soon as I close my eyes and drift away. The show goes on whether anyone's in the theater or not. In my dreams, the self is constantly making and remaking itself in recognizable or confusing patterns of meaning. Are my dreams true? Do they tell the truth that I refuse to admit? Regardless, it's obvious that my dreams have no filters—no ought, no should, no second chances—only power and possibility and the unvarnished reality of another world. Something is better than nothing.

But there's at least one other way of considering the life of meaning. Our lives are based on events, conversations, and relationships that happen every day. They happen whether they are planned or not, and most are not the result of our intent. We live storied lives and understand life itself as an unfolding of stories. We are brimming with stories stacked from toe to head, from the earliest to the most recent. They are mostly mundane, but often they are funny, tragic, or pivotal. There are too many stories held in consciousness to be accessible, and the overflow is stashed in the stacks of memory's library. These memories can be mapped by connecting the dots that make meaning out of the whole of life. Some are so deeply filed that they defy our ability to retrieve them until some trigger is pulled that suddenly and without conscious effort breaks loose a sliver of a memory or a sense of déjà vu. Such surprises come rushing toward us, seeking to be enticed to life. We should not be expected to believe all fragments of an experience in order for it to be verifiable, but they are what they are: broken bits of memory connecting us to some moment, some event that was at one time alive with wonder.

It is no small insight to recognize that big things happen at intersections. Life is filled with intersecting events and colliding moments. Lives are changed in such meetings. We take new directions and move forward with new impulses. We make decisions and then our decisions make us. There is the long life story, almost epic in nature, and there are the vignettes. We live from story to story episodically, like swinging on the monkey bars in the playground. This may or may not make sense until we step outside the moment and see the trail of stories that have delivered us to this moment, story after story as part of a larger whole making up the arc of life.

A single story or experience may or may not be a continuation of the story that preceded it and almost surely won't be suggestive of the next story. That's not how it works. But when our stories are seen as a whole, they become pointillistic vignettes in which even the pointless stories add something to the whole arc of our lives. Even the most common experiences make noble and purposeful what is agreeable: namely, that we live extraordinarily common lives. Many would suggest that these common lives are then made holy by their very commonness. At worst, we could say that they are *human* lives, as even in our humanity we may find great meaning. Our stories don't have to be courageous or noble or proof of any pudding. They will be a messy compilation of events in which occasionally we shine and in which we are often tarnished.

I know myself when I know my stories and savor them as mine. They are what is truthful about me even when I mangle them in "memory's unmade bed." The life of meaning is created when we re-experience our stories to mine them of deeper truth. Buried in each story is some treasure for us to discover. When we can accept that we are episodes of a larger story, the width and depth and sheer volume can be appreciated. We can even seek them like an explorer of a former world with a curiosity that drives us to either embrace them or seek to bury them.

All stories, small and large, significant or forgetful, contribute to the telling of anyone's story. It's a journey that can be traced from birth to childhood, through adolescence, and on to the long march of stages through adulthood until death marks life's end. The stories appear to be linear, one after the other, but at the same time they are cyclical, and the cycle of stories is commonly experienced by others whose stories are intersected. Linear life events, one after another, can purposefully take us from our beginnings, meander through the middleness of life, and come back to merge with one's endings. The challenge of life can be tracked as part of a large cycle of challenges, from dependence to independence to interdependence and eventually circling back to dependence. Middle adults call themselves the sandwich generation because often they are caring in some way for both their children and their parents. That reality puts both independence and interdependence under a harsh light as this generation is forced to navigate how to care for others without being ravaged by the complicated needs of those in their care.

Death can and will bring the cycle to conclusion in any of these stages, and it can sometimes be considered tragic for some while a relief for others. But does it necessarily mark the end? Or does the arc of life continue forward past death and beyond, sustained by others who bear bits and pieces of our lives? Do others keep the story alive? How long do the reverberations continue? Very few life stories have a lasting presence in the generations that follow. But admittedly, there are a few whose lives continue to draw our attention. For such people, their light shined so bright that it still glows, sustained in others who continue to view them as an aspirational legacy. For others, the light shined well on life, and that light may continue to shine for some time. But for most, the light has only a faint glow in family or friends, but it will surely diminish with the death of each person who had a front-row seat to your story.

If death does not define the end of the arc of one's life, what meaning does that give to those who are exploring their own stories? How is life's meaning understood to extend beyond one's existence? Can one embrace the full journey, even through decline and death, to see that life's echoes continue on in the lives of others? Some do not live across a full-orbed arc. They are the ones whose journey is interrupted, snapped off like a twig from the limb. But many do make the journey all the way to the end when their existence is claimed by the architect of life. One may or may not ascribe life to a particular understanding of the divine. With or without God, most see the logic that life has a structure or a path that is followed from beginning to end. It's a journey everyone makes: all who've come to completion and have stepped across the threshold of death, and all who are alive facing the challenges that seem to mark every person's journey.

Birth is how we assume the first stories began. We who have only the barest bones of consciousness have no say in the matter. Call it an act of the divine, call it a summons by life itself, but, in our conversion from a liquid life to an aerated world, we can only acknowledge that life mysteriously tipped over the first domino. In the splitting of cells and the orderly specialization of one cell from another, in the great mystery of life, we have come forward in our birth with a compelling life to live. Given the proper nurture, we cannot help fulfilling our purpose. We follow one moment with another, day after day, and we are engaged on the arc of life.

But is this when life begins? I'm not proposing the argument of the anti-abortion movement. I'm raising a question that goes deeper. When did I become a possibility and move closer to reality? When did the tumblers turn in my favor so that I would come into being? In a narrative understanding of life, I hear the faint beginnings of my own existence already evident in the stories of others, the stories of everyone who preceded me in this life—my parents, my grandparents, and the family lore we were raised on and joined at our birth. These stories form my prologue and initiate whole worlds of life's beginnings and all that follows. My prologue is not mine just yet, but I am in those stories nevertheless. How, you may wonder, are there life stories before our birth? How were our stories acti-vated before we were conceived? Only in midlife has this answer become clear. In midlife, one has new tools by which to address the questions of meaning with possible answers, or at least to come to terms with the ques-tions. While no one knew for certain of my coming, they were ready to welcome me well in advance of my arrival. I'm not a mystic about these things and am perhaps more innocent of how the tumblers were turning in order that I might emerge. My conception and birth occurred as the result of the conspicuous "slender threads" of how my parents met and were drawn together in the mystery of love.

All these gifts, the gifts of existence, the gifts of my story, and the whole arc of life, were mine at my birth, assigned to me as I made my first appear-ance. It was part of *a contract of life* received from the great mystery of creation, something that each of us receives in the gift of our existence. That contract was calculated as the miracle of vast sums of statistical data and cold, heartless science, of chemistry and biological processes; it came under the burden of our parents' highest hopes and their greatest fears and even as a part of holy whim and happenstance that we're only beginning to understand. The mystery of life's beginnings has passion and irrationality. It is the collective impulse of all creatures that exist, each woven into an inter-connected web that we are all drawn into as a condition of existence. Who can really assess what role is played by intuition, design, or sheer luck? How else can we explain things? Maybe your luck has been bad; likely, it's just been a mix of good and bad, like it has for the rest of us. God's will? Who can know? Whoever stakes a claim on God's will needs to be viewed with skepticism, as either someone who knows too little or assumes too much. I take some refuge in the idea of providence, but even that seems like a bold assumption. Providence is a faith assumption, but like most things about faith, it requires a leap. Maybe it's a leap of logic or even a leap taken in the dark. We make big assumptions in life; maybe this is not an unreasonable explanation. All of us need an ace up our sleeves, so why not providence?

The contract of life is a part of the deal one receives at birth.[36] We enter life with so many givens, all of which are determinative but also dynamic because of what we can do with them. Our contract of life takes into account our DNA—the physical blueprints with which we were made—our family history, and the ongoing story we joined by being birthed into these families, by the context in which we were born, and by the specific historical and geographical settings in which we were born.

I was born in the early 1950s in a white-flight suburb of Dallas. As a child of the suburbs, I had a particular upbringing of social structure and biases. I was born in the era when children were taught to crawl under their desks whenever the alarm was sounded. These realities helped write my contract in life. In the contract, we become co-creators with all the givens and refine them into opportunities for growth or advantage. We can also malinger with them and accept them as restraints that hold us back. They are the cards that are dealt. We can play them with skill and grace, or we can fold our hand and give in to them by seeing them as painful hobbles that restrict life and its opportunities. The contract of life is for some a broad-handed opportunity to grow and blossom, but for others it is an opportunity to live below the possibilities until life is squandered.

When one accepts the gift of life, one is drawn into a contract that includes the full realm of possibilities, worlds mostly unknown, accomplishments and failures. Only in looking over one's shoulder can the contract be understood. Only in understanding how the makings of life are constructed can one see that the contractual demands are really the ingredients one accepts in making life meaningful. Some would denigrate the contract of life as another failed defense of determinism, but this is not a true reading of how life is an invitation to accept the givens that are a part of our birth.

The story of the day my father and my mother met while living across the street from one another has convinced me that I have a prologue, a collection of stories that reach back in time before my birth and were key moments of the journey that led to my existence. Such stories are contained in the possibilities that were actualized in the actions, thoughts, passions, and willful acceptance of my parents' challenge of living their own lives. As a result of all those things, I came forward and began my journey. I came into being and was given my own life to live. From there the signposts measured and mapped my journey, signposts that were well worn by the journeys of others. While there's great mystery about how our lives are lived, one thing is certain: the arc continues past death in the lives of those who keep us alive in memory and thus keep us alive in their own trust.

We're all archaeologists of our stories,[37] mining them for meaning. The metaphor of archaeology seems apt as, in hearing our stories together, we are encouraged to draw on our observational powers, our persistence, and our delicate care, much like the archaeologist who uncovers one layer of earth at a time, looking for artifacts. Whether we tell our stories in a group or explore them alone, we are enticed to consider the stories within us as layered with depth and meaning. We're cartographers of a past life, making maps of the journey we've taken, connecting all the dots as we're able to understand them. These stories, these memories, are like broken shards, fragmented remembrances that memory has left to our care. How we see the pieces as a whole is an interpretive art that will uncover more of the story we tell whenever someone asks, "Who are you?" It might be useful to recognize that the narrative therapist regards this exploration with great optimism. The exploration of our stories as a whole is oriented toward hope, as the main character in these stories is assumed to be a courageous person, a victor, rather than someone who is pathologized as a victim. Storytellers are applauded for telling colorful stories rather than being people who lead pitiful lives. Anyone willing to explore their stories should be considered a highly developed person strong enough to engage a challenging journey of discovery.

Using the archaeologist's approach to explore our stories in a narrative manner means moving closer to the story rather than withdrawing. Stories that are "problem-saturated" likely indicate that we've steered away from the pain or the confusion of the story as it is held in our memories. We utilize an archaeologist's tools by taking a *not-knowing position* so that we can draw closer to the story's details and not make immediate, well-trod assumptions about what happened or what role we played or didn't play. Another tool from the archaeologist's toolbox is an open-ended curiosity that allows us to *ask curious questions*. These questions seek to widen the lens of understanding to include other hidden aspects of the story that we have dismissed or ignored. Finally, we are invited to adopt a *relentless optimism* that doesn't resort to pathologizing the story in a way that makes us the story's tragic victim due to poor judgment. In narrative practice, the central problem in a story full of problems is externalized from the story's actors. In this way, the problem itself can be understood without the need to unduly assign blame to ourselves or others as bad people who created the problem. This is not an attempt to dodge personal responsibility where it might reside; instead, the goal is to help us consider the effects of the problem without laying blame on certain characters. We are hard on ourselves. With the right tools of inquiry and a fresh perspective on our own problem-saturated stories, we can move across our arc of life even while bearing incredible pain and suffering. This alone is an argument for finding and developing a narrative community. (See essay 1, "How to Use this Book" for a detailed explanation of how a narrative group can work together to deepen their stories and, consequently, their lives.)

Story Starters: Emergence of Self

Here are some issues you might pursue from this essay:

• Memories are often built on the narrative structure of a beginning, a middle, and an end. As you read this section, what memory surfaced in your thoughts, triggered by this presentation? Can you see how that memory is constructed within the narrative framework? What type of memory is it?[38]

• Life happens at intersections. Memories are built on narrative events that occur at these intersections. As you look back at the stories that define you, do you recall an intersection in your life that is especially significant?

• Many scholars believe we use our memories, our narrative stories, to construct a meaningful sense of self, a larger story that is built out of these memories. As you read through this book about the arc of life, narrative clues may help you develop a conscious understanding of how you see yourself. What clues can you sense from this opening invitation to consider the meaning of your stories?

• The contract of life is a part of the deal one receives at their birth. Make a list of characteristics that were woven into your life story as part of your unique contract of life. While no one can fully categorize every element of this contract, people should be able to name major characteristics of their lives. (Refer to note 13 for an explanation of this contract.)

Journal

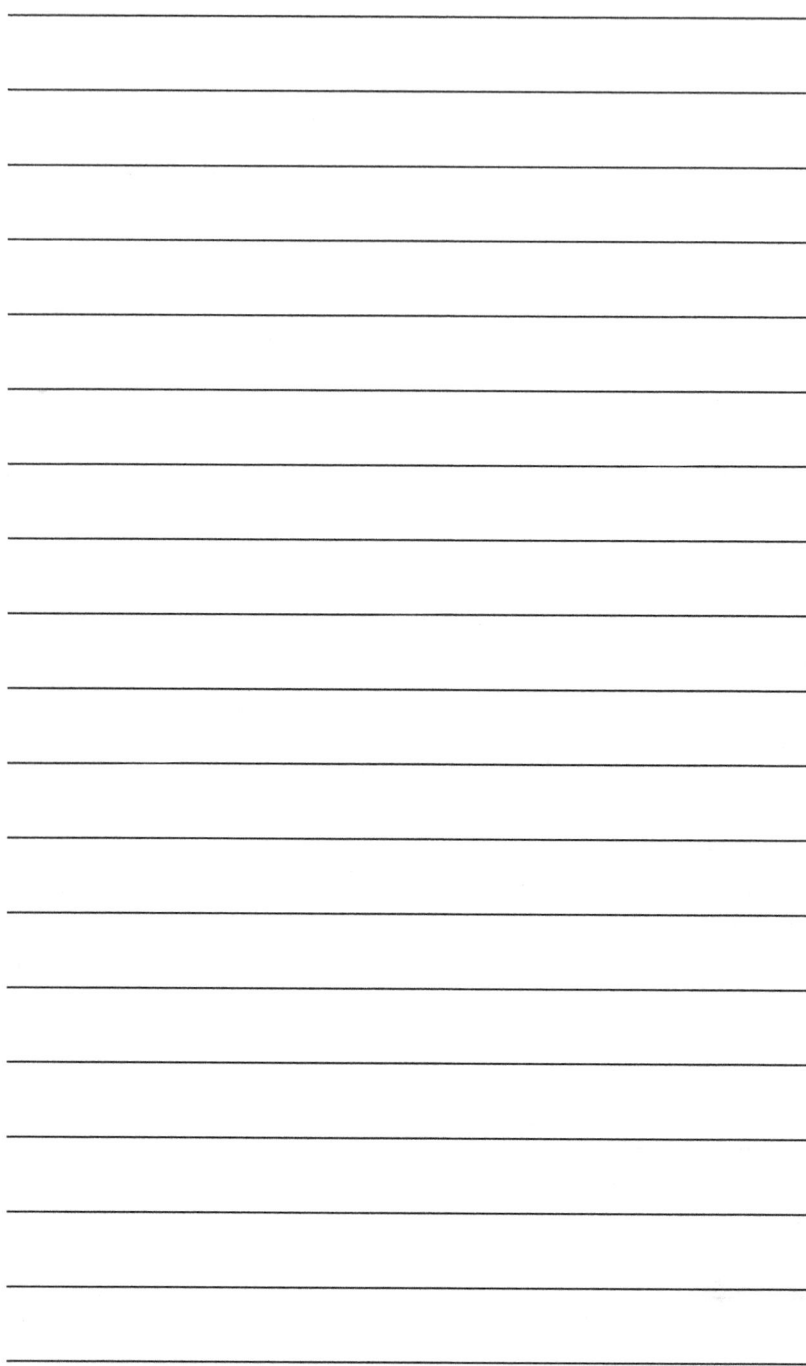

Prologue Stories– Exploring the Stories You Joined at Your Birth

Almost everyone assumes that their birth marks the beginning, which is indeed implied in the name we give this important moment. Our birth is the first domino tipped over. It's the house lights going down and the curtain rising. In a sequential way of describing life, we go to the beginning, to the day of our births, to tell our stories. Never mind the three quarters of a year we spent immersed inside our mothers' wombs where it was warm and dark. Never mind that we were traveling companions to our mothers all that time. Did your life begin at your birth, and, beyond that, does it end at your death? If we consider the arc of life, it has to have a beginning and an end, but is the arc of life bookended by birth and death?

Ask people about their births and they'll describe events they don't remember. They may begin by telling you facts, their birth date, height and weight, which hospital they were born in, or what the weather was like that day. Whatever story is told, it is borne from the stories of others who may or may not have even been there themselves. It was the most significant day of our lives, and we don't remember a blessed thing about it. We don't remember our mothers' cries or their profanity. All the grunting and sweating. We don't remember the masked nurses and doctors. We certainly don't remember being blinded by the intense lights. It's curious how we moved so suddenly from our aquatic existence to having our lungs emptied and then replaced with air. The doctors of old were full of tricks in such an exciting time. Why isn't this repressed memory driving us all to therapy? In that singular moment, it's the most remarkable, instantaneous transformation: we broke free from our buoyant oceanic life in the womb to gulp in our first gasp of air. From amniotic fluids to oxygen in the blink of an eye as we were held suspended upside-down. All of this was utterly amazing.

But it's important to realize there are stories that exist about you that don't include you because you had not yet arrived. The stories of others we consider predecessors of our own stories are included in what I am calling "the prologue stories." Some would suggest they are foreshadowing stories because they imply your presence as a silent, unseen character yet to be known—the possibility of someone, somewhere over the near horizon. These are the people and the stories that existed prior to your birth, but they contain the earliest fragments of your story. If all of us are woven into a complicated and inclusive web of stories, how can we sort them out? How is my story not woven into your story in some six degrees of separation? It's apparent to me that if we are to find meaning in these stories, we will need to do some editing by adding value to the people who are the vital connections from your beginnings until now. There are others embedded in all these stories, but at this point their importance is meaningless to your sense of identity. We will leave them out as a courtesy to our ability to hold these stories in orbits that touch our own experiences of life.

Prologue stories are the ones you join at your birth, the stories that were already in motion before you arrived to join them. "You were just a glint in your parents' eyes," we often say with a wink. Our intention is to signify that while they may not have been thinking of you in particular, they were at least thinking the thoughts that created you. Prologue stories are all the stories you can claim as your own because they are the stories of all the people you encountered upon your birth. The people who populate these stories may be completely agnostic to the role they will play in your story, but nevertheless they are there. Life is broad enough to include them, and there's no denying they are a part of the big picture of how you came to be and how you joined them in the living of their stories. However you arrived, you are inextricably woven into their stories.

To get a clearer picture of this community of stories you joined at your birth, do this exercise: Imagine a photo being taken at your birth. It snaps in your brain through the lens of your eyes as you lie wrapped in a warm blanket during your first moments outside your mother's womb. This picture captured in time should include all the people who are anticipating your arrival and will become a part of your life. Since this is a fanciful photographic exercise meant to help you claim them all, give yourself license to place them all in the photograph—whether they were present in the hospital or not. Include all the characters in your prologue (that is, the stories you join at your birth) in this photograph. Don't leave anyone out. Bring them all to this moment so they can join the group pose. Imagine they are all peering at the newborn you, wide-eyed with wonder. When you blink your eyes and snap the picture, who is there?

From that photograph, create a three-dimensional image of the stories of the key players you see in your prologue. Think of your parents and grandparents and the families from which they came. Think of the key events that took place prior to your birth, events that, unbeknownst at the time, were an integral part of the slender threads of your beginnings.[39] Include important neighbors or friends. Whether or not they know why they are there, place them in time and space in this composite memory of all those who were present at your beginning. Like you, all of them live on an arc of time. Imagine that their arcs and their stories are now a part of your story because life has drawn them into your story. Their stories are joined with yours as you build your own life.

If life is understood narratively—if we accept that the journey of our lives is mapped by our stories, whether they come in the form of individual vignettes or are segments of long, expansive story sequences—we typically understand that the clock on our existence begins at our births. Our personal narratives begin immediately from that beginning and continue onward with each new day. "From beginning to end," we claim. We are brimming with such stories. One of life's tasks is to find or make meaning of all these stories. We vacillate between experience and reflection, back and forth from one moment to the next. Whenever we're not actively experiencing something, we're thinking about what a particular experience might mean. Philosophers and psychologists have noted this swinging pendulum of how we immerse ourselves in the living of life and how, at the same time, we seek to make meaning of life.

In truth, our stories didn't begin at our birth; rather, we joined a larger story composed of others' stories, likely anchored by our parents' stories. They were living in the stream of their own narratives when we entered it. There is a rich diversity of family types—two parents, one parent, foster parents, grandparents (every other human combination), who brought with them all the histories of their own families, their friends, and the experiences that drew them together. A part of our search for meaning is to fully examine our origins and to add meaning to our own existence by taking into account this diversity because we emerged from the web of their stories. Their history became the basis for our own history. In truth, their experiences became the shape of our own stories, and we "borrowed" from them our first concepts of self before our own stories were ever known or understood. We emerged with an identity forged from those narratives before our own stories were formed and embraced. Our personal stories joined theirs, already in motion, like jumping onto a moving merry-go-round.

The life stories of those we joined at our birth were both independent and connected. Our creation may have been brought about by the interconnectedness of their bodies in the act of procreation, but their stories were also at work. Every strand of their stories was woven into their coming together to form us. From a narrative perspective, their storied worlds represent everything meaningful about them—their memories, their families of origin, their hopes, and their dreams. All of these were present in our conception. Everything was in place for our arrival. The interconnected polarities of individual and communal are always at work in our stories: it's "me," and it's "us." Frank Stagg calls this interconnection "the polarity of solitude and solidarity, individuality and community."[40] Polarities describe the outer boundaries, but the experiences of life are mostly lived between the poles. We first ground our existence in the larger narratives of our parents, other older siblings, and extended family. But then, as we grow, our own stories emerge and eventually stand on their own. We become a self and are less merged with our families of origin. Eventually, we grow more individualized. The extent to which we move toward complete individualization is arguable; the framework of our lives is continually shaped by the community of family and friends that shaped us from the beginning. We move in life through a cycle of various shades of dependence to independence (perhaps better understood as interdependence), and, if we live long enough, we will journey back to dependence as our autonomy and self-control give way to our need for others.

All these experiences, all these memories that link our parents to their past, are only available to us in limited ways, although, admittedly, they are mostly hidden from us and must be delivered to us in the form of the stories other people share with us. Wisdom comes with maturity, and only later in life can we put the fragments of our parents' and other family members' stories into focus. Stories told to us in our childhood must be revisited when we're older and able to understand the deeper meanings. By midlife we become as curious as kittens, finally seeing the larger facets of our family stories and beginning to understand how they have been the shaping forces of our own stories. We come to the place where we see others' stories as our stories, incorporated into our own. It's a jigsaw puzzle where one segment is linked to others and then to other groups of memories until a larger, clearer picture emerges.

How, you may wonder, are there life stories before our birth? How were our stories activated before we were conceived? Only in midlife does this question become clear. While no one knew for sure of my coming, big players in my life were ready to welcome me well in advance of my arrival. No one knew whether I would be a boy or a girl, but that didn't seem to matter to most, as they were readying themselves to widen the reach of the family to make room for me.

In the season of her dying, my mother told me a story that helped me understand that the houses in which three of my grandparents lived were across the corner from one another. I learned that a young man had come home from the war and was taking art classes at the nearby college. In the house across the street, my maternal grandparents were supporting their daughter as she took business courses. This young sailor was on top of his mother's roof repairing wind-blown shingles, and he looked down on the dirt path along the road and saw a shapely young woman walking to her own house just across the street. I don't know who spoke to whom, whether there was a whistle to get her attention or just a called-out greeting. I know nothing of what was said, who said what, or much of anything. Nevertheless, it was then, in that single moment, that the man who was to become my father and the young woman who was to become my mother first met.

No one misses the point that my rendering of their meeting is vague and necessarily a fictionalized version of what might have really happened. But since both my mother and father are gone, I can tell the story to fit my own needs. My mother told me a version of this story, and I've taken the poetic license to make my own meaning. Like every broken memory, the facts are burnished with age. The memory is sketchy and has surely been edited so it may or may not have resembled this telling. In fact, the true telling will never be known, as both of my parents lived out a long life together, and the story, as they say, went with them to the grave. "As it should be" is the proper response. This is the story my mother finally told me toward the end of her life, and in the dying light of her memory, everything was contained in that moment. Three sons were held fast in that single encounter, merely needing time and opportunity to make their appearance. This story is emblematic of other stories that all combine in some grand mystery to tell the beginnings of my story before I ever made my appearance. Before the arc of my life had its official beginning, my story was told in the lives of my father and my mother and their families. This story of a young man and a young woman meeting and speaking to one another is not my story alone but is a shared story between my two brothers and me. Each of us has a place to occupy in how that story brought us into existence and into relationship with the young woman and man and also with one another. How could it be otherwise? My mother's memory was held in her heart across the arc of her own life until, in generosity, she told it to me as the waning light was dimming. I suspect she felt the story needed to be shared. I don't remember ever hearing of it until then.

That one memory has convinced me that I have a prologue, a collection of stories that reach back in time before my birth and were key moments of the journey that led to my existence. These are the stories contained in the possibilities that were actualized in the actions, thoughts, passions, and willful acceptance of my parents' challenge of living their own lives. As a result of all those things, I came forward and began my own journey. From there the signposts measured and mapped my journey—signposts that were not unique to me alone, signs that were well worn by the journeys of others. The journey crosses the arc of life through childhood, adolescence, and the ever-changing stages of adulthood until it comes to the end, when death claims us. While there's a great mystery about what happens to us after we die, one thing is certain: the arc continues on in the lives of those who keep us alive in memory and thus keep us alive in their own trust.

My stories were interwoven with those of my parents, and it is difficult to imagine how their stories were outside of and distinct from my own. I lived in a family beehive of stories that embraced mine and predated mine. How did these melded stories exist without me? I had no notion they ever did, but it must be admitted that I was grafted into their ongoing stories both in my conception and at my birth. Curious . . . was I always there? Even before I was conceived, did I already exist in this web of stories? Was there some unopened door of mystery where I existed even before there was ever a thought that I might join the stream of stories being lived and experienced?

But my story was widened because, a decade later, a third son was born. His stories of childhood were completely different because he missed the preschool days spent on the set of his older brothers' stories (to be explained in Essay Four). His stories were just as tender but different. As a part of his prologue, I can testify that the family was fully engaged in preparing for his arrival. Before he was born, names for two genders were chosen in the likelihood that he would be one or the other. With two sons already, my mother's hope for a girl was palpable.

My parents did not include my older brother and me in their discussion of the need to find a larger house, as adult conversations about such matters hovered above our heads and beyond our grasp of knowing. They sold the two-bedroom post-WWII frame house where the four of us had lived and bought a new, from-scratch brick home in a new subdivision. We had no yard, the trees were barely twigs, and all new additions to the houses were built on the black North Texas soil called "gumbo" (to describe what it looked like when it rained). Only recently, these newly platted suburban streets had been farmland before being sold off to developers. It seemed that everyone in the neighborhood was cut out of the same cloth. Two parents, two cars, two jobs, often two or more children. All our neighbors were strapped for money, but they were filled with ambition and had faith that they were moving up the ladder. I remember visiting the street of new houses that were being built by a well-known suburban developer and walking through the skeleton frame of what would become our new house. I recall my parents as prospective homeowners, picking the color of bricks and carpeting, choosing the floor plan, etc. The permanence of a brick house was a sure sign of our middle-class prosperity, since the post-war home we were living in was a frame house with shiplap siding. We watched our new house go up, and then we moved. We didn't move far, but we did attend a brand new school built because of the widening city limits that now included what had previously been rural land. In fact, I only attended this new school for one year, as another new school was being built that was closer to our new home. I attended two years of junior high in a well-established school, but in my third year, I once again helped open a new junior high that was centrally located on our city's west side where the new elementary schools were constructed.

My older brother and I were halfway to high school as we watched our mother grow with this expected infant, and we waited to see who might come join our stories. Like our parents, we lived with the mystery of whether this would be a little brother or a little sister. I can't tell my younger brother's stories, just my own. "He" could have been a "she," a wish our mother bore at some inner level of her heartfelt desire. Our mother's deep inner dream for herself was that she was created to be the mother of a girl, and all three of us failed in fulfilling her motherly desire. Absent her own daughter, she doted on our sister-cousin to fulfill that wish. None of us boys were jealous of that, as I believe we understood that our sister-cousin filled a need in our mother we were unable to fill. The fact that our mother was a superb mother of boys kept us secure in her love. But at least two of us, my younger brother and me, both had female names at the ready in case we were daughters. Significant to us all was the decision our mother made to suspend her work in the family-run insurance company so she could stay home to raise our younger brother and also to stabilize our home so the two of us older boys would not be neglected. Our lives as a family were growing busier and busier, although the chaos was mild in comparison to today's young families.

Prologue stories are meant to capture how the anticipation of your arrival was thought of and understood by those whose stories you joined. Prologue stories are as truthful for those whose stories we joined at our birth as they are for us. Likely, it's only in adult maturity that we can explore them as stories about others as well as stories about ourselves. Part of exploring the self is seeking to understand how the stories of important people who were at our births were living their own stories, animated by their own dreams and altered by their successes and failures. All I can do is see is my own birth and how the world opened up to let me in. Upon my younger brother's arrival and my own birth, we joined the stories of the family that brought us into existence. It was as if we had been there all along.

The flow of life brings people in and out of our lives. Some of my prologue stories were diminished in memory at the death of those with whom I had shared a journey for even the briefest of times. The generation of great-grandparents was dying in the same season that I was born, and my limited memories of them are a thin recall just beyond memory's sure reach. Some of that memory came as I heard the stories of my grandparents who were grieving the loss of their parents. Family tales still included these great-grandparents as a sign of their importance to the family that I only partially knew. A quest to widen the reach of my memory to include them is increasingly difficult, as by the time we wish to locate them in our prologue stories, those who knew them have also died or disappeared. We are left with the dream state they inhabited but are largely beyond any efforts to recover them. They are shadowy figures who exist on the outer fringes of our stories, if they exist at all, just beyond our reach to remember. Today, particularly as my brothers and I have gone through the remains of our parents' earthly possessions, this generation that was leaving as we were arriving are kept partially alive in a handful of photographs that prompt me with the visual memories of them in a vague way. Nevertheless, the arc of life was already visible as one generation was fading into the past while a generation of the future was emerging, and now I'm living in the wisdom of seeing the whole arc of life from their faded memories to their sense of hopefulness that the next generation was emerging to take their place.

My great-grandparents are mostly mute figures in my earliest stories. They are people remembered in fragments, likely shaped more by family photographs than by my own memory, but I doubt the factual nature of those remembrances as they were so brief and I was too young to have captured much of their stories other than their poses for family snapshots. Whatever memories exist in my mind are populated by family figures to whom I've attached my own meaning. They exist in my thoughts mostly in biblical terms from the Hebrew poets: "For a thousand years in your sight are like yesterday when it is past, or like a watch in the night. You sweep them away; they are like a dream, like grass that is renewed in the morning; in the morning it flourishes and is renewed; in the evening it fades and withers."[41] The morning mist or the fleeting illusion of dreams are apt metaphors for these memories that are just outside my reach. Prologue memories place them in time and space and in my stories, but there's too little actual recall for them to be set firmly in my self-understanding. What of them remains, perhaps unrecognized by me but attributable to them nevertheless? What habits of being do I demonstrate? What values are embedded in my way of seeing the world? What physical traits of theirs do I possess? Am I of this stock, or am I living an altogether different life?

In a narrative approach to understanding life, particularly in considering the arc of life, we come to recognize that our stories do not begin at birth. There are trace elements of earlier stories that we must consider if we are to take it all in, every fragment and every sense in which we inhabit a body and come to consciousness. Birth stories are wide and varied, and each includes the width and breadth of life's possibilities that color the stories with amazingly unique and utterly human details.

I was born fifty weeks after my older brother, who was born nine months after our parents were married. That's two births inside of two years with three months to spare. My older brother and I were grown with children of our own before we had a generational meeting of the three brothers and our spouses in which we conducted a sibling math class. Our mother would have been too embarrassed to join us in this exercise, so these calculations occurred in her absence. Specifically, we wondered, did our mother have sex with our father ahead of the wedding? She raised us so that our provincialism about sex outside of marriage was apparent. The most scandal we could conjure was that our older brother was conceived on the honeymoon. That might imply several conclusions, all mythic in nature. The most obvious would be that our parents knew very little if anything about birth control. No one would accuse our father of not knowing the simple facts of life, but what about our mother? If actions counted as indicators of knowledge, one could assume neither of them knew much since two boys were born inside of twenty months. So were both boys unexpected surprises? These explanations were never explored in true honesty with our parents. We didn't ask and they didn't tell. All we have are calendar dates and a few other clues.

Later in early adulthood, my mother offhandedly mentioned that when I was born, she was hoping for a girl. She even had my name picked out, ready to add some pink to her life. Our younger brother was conceived nine years later, so all of us have assumed that the three of us were surprises and that at least two of us were disappointing to our mother because of our gender. We recognized that there was nothing personal in her preferences; she made the best of it by loving us despite the fact that we were boys. I was an adult before she gave me these clues. I suppose she didn't want me to think she wasn't happy with me for being a boy. I also suppose my mother was spare in giving me other details that might be included in this book. If so, she was wise.

The streams of location and time and culture and other stories are flowing through time in these collective waters. Your stream has been flowing through time until your time to arrive appeared. You did not create this stream, and it was not created just for you, but in no uncertain terms, in the mystery of happenstance, that stream is yours. We are the combined byproducts of people and events, culture and history, time and location that were all present at our births. All of this is your particularized story. You were born at a particular place and time, born into a particular family arrangement. Your birth is like any other birth in most respects, but it is also uniquely yours. You were born in the struggle of a mother who labored to deliver you. Consequently, if you were lucky, you were also raised within a healthy family arrangement—who labored to bring you to independence and maturity, two challenging qualities for anyone. In the end, this is a matter of someone who cared enough to see that you became you, or as Grady Nutt would say, "I am a person of worth, created in the image of God."[42] All factors of place and time are windows into the culture in which we are birthed. And all of these factors are actively involved in shaping the formation of ourselves. To accept the givens is a convenient truth, as they are how the contract of life must be lived and that we must accept, but is the grist of late-night discussions in college to explore how our stories might have created new lives we did not live.

The river of life you stand in is part of the one that was flowing at your conception. It contains the stories of all who have been a part of your coming into existence, your mother and father and all their kin. The streams in which they stand are part of your stream. The stories that brought them to one another and eventually to you are deep channels in this stream— you with them, and with all that are connected to them. That river of life is rich with meaning, but most of it flows by us unrecognized. The value of a narrative curiosity means that we are invited to go backward in time to analyze and study all that has flown by in days when we cannot capture it all. To take this journey, we likely need co-travelers, others who perhaps shared the journey, others with whom we might exercise our imaginations and our curiosities.

We stand knee-deep in a river that flows out of time immemorial.
The river of life was flowing on its own long before we arrived.
The river carries all that has gone on before,
beyond ancient memory or record.
We are a part of the stream for a bit of time—
Everything before us goes into the making of us.
We are formed by the river and the river gives us life.
We flow in waters that carried our past forward.
It moves and gurgles their stories, sounds that echo our own.
The river flows on . . .

Story Starters: Prologue

The prologue season is about the times prior to your birth in which your presence was implied even though you were not yet born. This would be the time when your birth was anticipated in some known or even unknown way. You were implied but not fully present. Prologue stories give you a chance to explore how you joined the stories of others. You were not present for any experiences of life, but, looking back, you can sense how you were present in some suggestive way. With a generous imaginative effort, you can acknowledge how others were living their lives when you joined them at your birth. The stories of all these others who welcomed you at your birth have lived in stories upstream of your own. Some of these people are silent and unseen but present nonetheless. You emerged to weave your story into their many stories. This is the richness of the community we have joined.

Story starters are a collection of story seedlings, suggested topics to help you see your life across the arc of time and to help you consider how prologue stories are the stories of others you joined at your birth. Here are some possibilities you might engage from this essay, "Prologue Stories: Exploring the Stories You Joined at Your Birth":

• **Prior Family Life.** Do you know how your parents were living prior to your conception? Were they together in some recognizable form? Where did they live? How old were they, and can you imagine them at that age? Were there older siblings already alive? What about the extended families of your parents? What were they doing at this stage of their lives? Were they working? If so, what were they doing? Are you aware of their dreams or wishes in life? What role did your birth play in those dreams?

• **Anticipation of Birth.** Did your parents anticipate and plan your birth? How do you know this? Or did your birth surprise them? Interviewing other family members could help you fill in the missing gaps.

• **Your Parents' Family Life.** How do you describe your mother's family? Your father's family? What did those families look like at the time of your conception? Can you imagine your grandparents as middle-aged adults and your parents as young adults, perhaps just out of adolescence? Are there family photographs that help you imagine them at the age they were at the time of your conception?

• **Preexistent Stories.** What stories exist in the family lore (those stories shared as part of the identity of the family) and include you from before your birth?

• **Preparing for Essay Four.** Recall your stories of childhood and select one according to the questions suggested at the end of the next session. If you are part of a group, come ready with a story to explore.

Journal

_____

_____

_____

_____

_____

_____

_____

_____

_____

_____

_____

_____

_____

_____

_____

_____

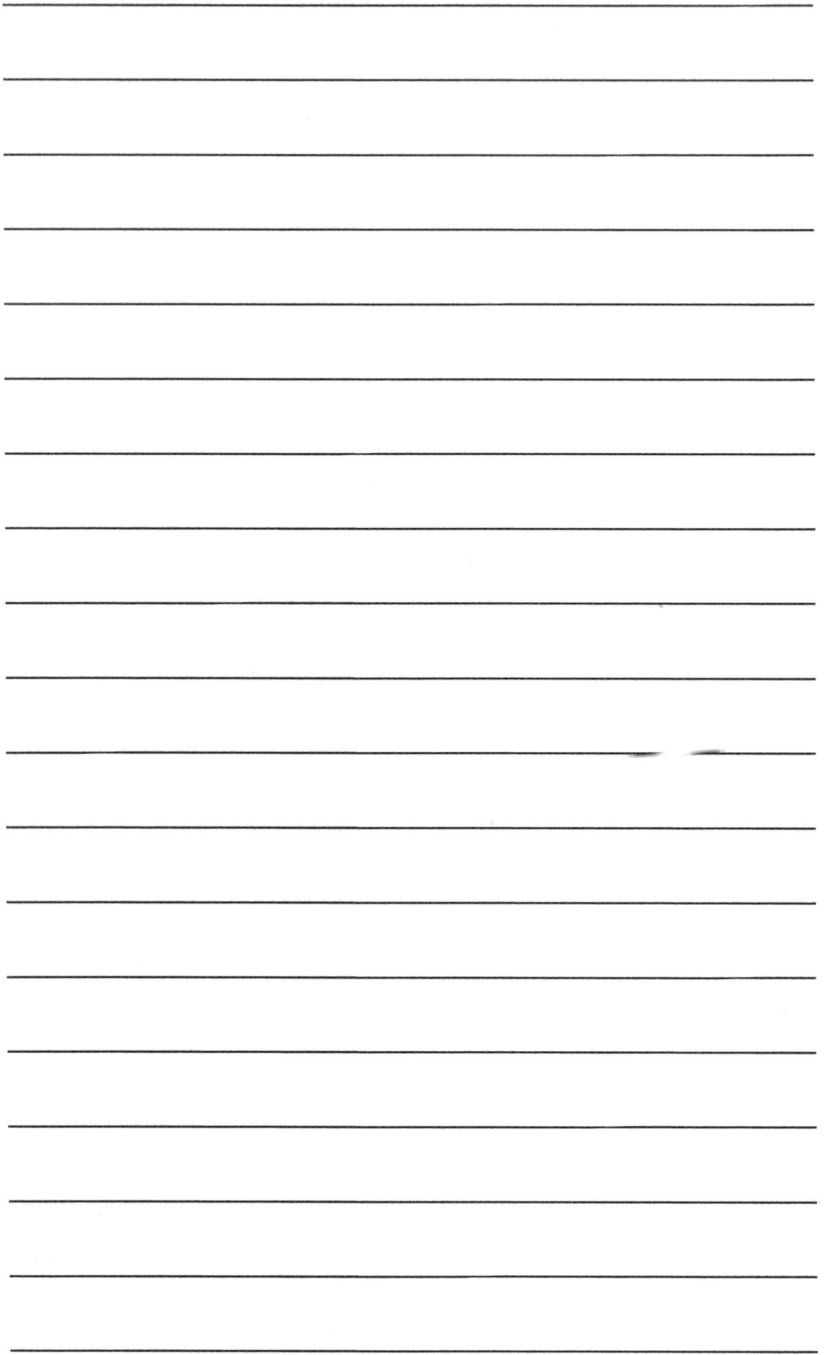

Childhood– The First Decade

I am the one with eyes wide open, mesmerized by whatever crosses my gaze. I'm mostly captivated by faces, shiny objects, animals of all kinds, and other children. I am capable of the widest range of basic emotions but resist emotional complexities; I can only seem to hold one feeling at a time. When I have one feeling engaged, I'm all in. If I'm sad, I'm bawling like a, well, you know. I can laugh my head off. Loud family arguments and tension can scare me. Walk out of the room and leave me alone and I'll melt down in sobbing fear. I am you and you are me and I need you in order to be me.

I have power over the behavior of big adults, especially old people who cannot control themselves around me. They want to cuddle with me, nuzzle my neck and face, and touch my skin as if they've never held a child in their lives. I bedazzle them with my personality until I grow bored of them. When I get tired, I doze off.

My mother's presence dominates my world. She is my first provider, my north star, my whole sense of being. She is my warmth, my nurture, my feeding, my cleaning. I need the same from my father—the embrace of his rough hands, the smell of his body different from my mother, but like home for me, in order to know trust. Their sameness and continuity are the essence of assurance. Their presence and love is an ever-present source of stability that gives me confidence to be me. I don't know it now, but I hit the jackpot. It's a numbers game that not everyone enjoys. One good parent gives me enough to move forward with enough chips in my corner to make a go of life. The parental combinations are mind-blowing as I learn in school from my buddies who have one or another parent, two moms, two dads, grandparents. Three square meals a day, a roof over my head, and love, love, love are what I need most.

I am the one doing the impersonations with my eyes and my nose, smiling, and practicing what others say or sing. I don't need words because even my gibberish is a language unto itself. Even before I say a word, I'm practicing, learning from whoever gets in my face and talks to me. Who's gibbering to whom? I wonder. I could take this show on the road.

Not quite fluent in the language of jokes, I love playing games. Fingering my toes and making animal noises are my first lessons. I am so musically inclined that even if I don't know the song, I can make one up. Once I can stand on my wobbly legs, I take off to explore my world. I can run and skip and dance as I cross a room on unsteady legs. Being only two feet tall, it's easy to get lost in a crowd, but there's always some big person who will stoop to tousle my hair or pick me up or try to get me to pay attention to them. I have favorite books already and want to read them every night. If you skip a page, I'll know. I can hear you read the same story to me every night and not be bored.

I am a seriously curious thinker but don't know how to handle the world of metaphors. You say it and I believe it. Not to be dismissed, my brain is constantly raising questions for adults to answer. I'm an unabashed philosopher wondering how the world is wired and what it all means, thinking outside the box on almost any issue.

Because I'm such an adventurer, I have a tendency to race full tilt out of control until, inevitably, I crash and fall and skin my knees and elbows, or even hit some unforgiving object with my head. I cry with tears running off my face so that when I suffer, all others suffer too.

I can swim naked in a tub of warm water until my toes and fingers wrinkle. Wrapped in a warm towel, I break free and streak around the house in pure joy. Then into my jammies and to bed where I demand a book or a story to calm my thoughts until my eyelids are too heavy to hold open. Stories at bedtime are one of my favorites . . . the cuddling, the soothing voice animating my storybook, slipping off into sleep. Comfort and joy!

I am the one who may have cried on my first day of school but then came to learn that school was just another adventure, a drama on another stage, where friends are made and where the teacher's praise is worth working for. Each grade is a challenge with its metrics and measurements and tales of heroic characters. I say the Pledge of Allegiance from memory and have an entire songbook of songs to sing. I learn the sophisticated games where rules govern our play.

My world expands every day. I am a sponge of discovery, mindful of an ever-expanding world. Every day is an open door. I step over the threshold into a new world with wonder, embracing and savoring it with gratitude.

✦

From a recurring dream, I have a faint memory of what it felt like to be buoyant as a child. I remember what it felt like to live so lightly that you could literally float and not be bound by gravity. I can still get in touch with my ancient, long-buried memories of those days when I would be weightless to the world's troublesome realities. The four members of our family lived in a suburban, two-bedroom, post-WWII house so simple that it would seem it could be built over a long weekend by a gaggle of volunteers. My older brother and I shared the second bedroom, and all of us shared the single bathroom. In honesty, I don't remember much about sharing a room for eight years with my brother. I know our single shared closet was only a bit wider than the closet door itself yet seemed adequate for our clothes and a handful of other personal belongings. We must have had a chest of drawers and crammed the rest of our things under our beds. In comparison to most children today, we had surprisingly few possessions.

Perhaps my mind has polished memories of events that never occurred, but it doesn't really matter how I've reclaimed them, does it? The important part is that I can. There are a few other memories, but they seem insignificant now, minuscule details that add nuance to my childhood. Childlikeness is a good gift I'm rediscovering as an adult. We're much too encrusted with adulthood to live in those memories for long, so I consider it a good thing that I can remember anything at all, even if the glimpses only come sweetly as unbidden reminders of a lost world. For many adults, burying this childlikeness is the price we pay to grow up, to be taken seriously, to assume the burden of maturity. Can we be both serious and childlike? Can our childlike curiosity be nurtured as a form of adult inquiry? Or is our childhood sacrificed on the altar of growth, a necessary death that we give up all too easily?

It's the state of childhood that interests me these days. I'm curious how the many insignificant happenings shaped my life. I'm interested in those forgotten moments that have survived time and distance until they bubble up from the netherworld of memory. Memory is warmed by how I was loved and nurtured by my parents and others in my extended family and by being my brother's shadow. I fully embrace the reality that "nothing happened." Sure, I was once bitten by a vigilant black dog in front of a neighboring house and had to lower my pants in front of my friend's mother because we couldn't pull my jean leg high enough to check out my wounds. How did we escape the business of hiring a lawyer? There are a handful of other memories from childhood, but in the end, I can say with truthfulness that nothing happened, or at least nothing that didn't happen to every other kid in some way. All that nothingness . . . did it amount to anything meaningful? Absolutely.

Psychologists have dedicated great energy into thinking about the period from birth forward under the general umbrella we call "childhood." We know when it begins, but when does it bend around to become adolescence? Is this change fluid, or is it fixed by certain signs? And within childhood, are there developmental signposts that are observed to indicate certain stages? Traditional Freudian approaches describe micro-phases that are best understood from a psychologist's perspective. The rest of us look across these stages more perfunctorily through event-based stories.

From a narrative vantage point, perhaps using Alfred Adler's interest in our earliest childhood memory would be a good place to begin. Adler's practice of asking clients about their earliest memories came about in the belief that such recollections provide a window into the present moment, often mirroring currently held convictions and attitudes. No one seems to hold more than a handful of these memories, and some claim that their earliest memories aren't all that early. The body of forgotten memories are what Adler called "infantile amnesia." These stories are usually simple in structure, and despite that simplicity they are understood dynamically and considered projective, that is, they are projections of current concerns. Imagine the frustration of the older sister leaning down to the ear of the newborn brother and whispering, "Tell me . . . what's it like? It's been so long and I've already forgotten."

Adler's use of early childhood memories was intended to provide a glimpse into the unspoken inner world of the client. Such memories are reconstituted as a focused sensory memory. They operate like a wormhole connecting the present with some remembered image that is "remembered" in a way that mirrors the present concern. Adler felt that there were no chance memories and believed that, out of the countless impressions, one would select to remember only those perceived, even darkly, to have bearing on one's current situation. These first memories give an insight into a person's fundamental view of life, a first crystallization of one's orientation toward life.[43] Life does not consist of an endless series of disconnected events or memories. Rather, the arc of life is a mosaic of events and the subsequent reflections on them. Adler and others writing in psychology assert that their views are descriptions of a theory of expression. Memories and how they operate in our thoughts help us "maintain an orientation through time, to rehearse our understanding of the fundamental issues of life, and to provide ourselves with reminders of the reliability of our convictions."[44]

From the cradle where we take our first nap to our first existential angst over whether we will get our next meal to those moments of exploring our fresh, new bodies, we have a series of firsts, one right after another, until we realize the beauty of repeated regularity that can itself be comforting. If we cry, there's the possibility we will be picked up and soothed. It's our first magic trick in the behavioral training of our parents. If we cry with full body and voice, someone, maybe one of our parents, will come to our rescue. Helplessness is its own education, as we learn through trial and error. In the end, we have more control than we can imagine or fully comprehend.

Theorists of varying schools of thought have made meaningful maps either in service to Erik Erikson or others who have framed how life has a trajectory, follows a path, and comes to a conclusion. The question all these writers raise eventually embraces the idea of meaning. What meaning can be derived from our early years when nothing happened? To hold these memories, to revere them in spite of their insignificance, we must embrace aspects of early experiences beyond the reach of the trace memories of our childhoods. We do this by immersing ourselves in the stories of those who lived upstream of us. I've come to see our memories as inhabited by significant people who were actively at work in relationship to us, loving us, giving us their attention, and showering us with affirmation. I understand that not every child has these gifts, and so the value of those relationships may vary from significant to meaningless. Pastoral theologian John Claypool used the metaphorical language of Hebrew faith to label this stage of life as "anointed with delight."[45] Claypool claimed that each child should be blessed with a sense of personal worth, something of "a blessing for being." This is usually a process that overflows out of those who are closest to the child—parents, grandparents, aunts or uncles, or almost any elder who has an intent of giving an intentional blessing to the child, whether or not that intent is fully comprehended for how deeply that blessing moves the child toward wholeness. Those who have had someone shine a positive light on them are truly blessed. Those with someone who accepts the power of this kind of influence receive the gift of being. Children can grow toward life without these kinds of people, but it's clearly a bonus when someone sends these signals to us as we're growing up.

Psychologist Myron Madden explored the relationships that exist whereby a child receives a blessing for being: "A genuine self-acceptance must be started at some point outside the self; it must come from another who has been able in turn to accept healing from his [sic] own broken-ness."[46] This kind of affirmation often comes from within the family, but it is also received from some other influential person outside the family itself. The affirmation of being affirms us as we are, not as we would like to be or even as we hope to become. It is a blessing for right now in the current moment. The power of this kind of affirmation can be understood as inherent in creation itself. One is blessed in creation as a gift from the universe.

Our parents were given this first opportunity to envelop us in affirmation in their role as life creators. In the mystery of new beginnings, we were created in their act of passion with one another.[47] This gift of life is ours for existence. The gift of affirmation, according to Madden, comes in creation not as a reward for good performance. There is nothing done that triggers this affirmation. We are blessed for our being, and that gives us the foundation on which we add confidence-building events where we can shape our lives and accept the adventure that life can be. This kind of affirmation is like a blood transfusion, perhaps understood as a life transfusion as an adult—an elder to us—passes along affirmation, which has the power to ignite a sense of destiny in us.

Blessing only knows one tense: now. There is no past tense or future tense to a blessing. Only now does it wield its power. This affirmation is not about something done, some accomplishment in the past, or something one might do in the future. A blessing is a simple affirmation for being. It is a restoration to wholeness. It is a powerful platform of affirmation for one to receive, and its effects are breathtaking. Madden is clear that this blessing is meant to energize children beyond the family, giving them the confidence needed to cut the cords that bind them in emotional dependence on parents, siblings, and the extended family. What happens when the confidence of affirmation is not granted? Novelist Pat Conroy expressed it this way: "I longed for their approval, their applause, their pure uncomplicated love for me, and I have looked for it years after I realized they were not even capable of letting me have it."[48] Perhaps for most children it is feast or famine, as we all come from a staggering variety of home settings.

Some parents are there for a while and then are absent for other periods of time. Parents can be amazing givers of blessing, and if they aren't, there are grandparents or other adult figures who can fill in the gaps.

We begin life as fragile creatures, helpless and dependent. So the challenge of existence is to learn to exist on our own. From the moment of our birth, we are engaged in a process of separation and individuation. Our first separation is from the womb. Then we move steadily with our parents in successive stages of separation, breaking free from total dependency to living an independent/interdependent life. What we don't know until later is that our parents and our families of origin are our partners in these stages of separation, simultaneously experiencing their own sense of loss and growth.

D. W. Winnicott, British pediatrician and psychoanalyst, offered a generous concept of parenting aimed at the heart of most parents' anxiety as he promoted the idea of "the good enough mother."[49] In considering the efforts of the mother (or any other caregiver), Winnicott observed how the typical caregiver is focused on the immediate needs of the infant, giving up their own needs in order to meet the demands of the young one. This means the caregiver is tied into every moment and meets the incessant demands of the infant, often to the neglect of the needs of the caregiver. As time goes by, without even planning to do this, the caregiver frustrates the infant, who must learn that the world does not stop spinning on its axis when the infant cries. By allowing the child longer and longer moments in which to express a need through crying or some other signal, the parent is helping the child to calm down, knowing that it may take longer than "immediately" for the child's needs to be met. The child learns that the parent or other caregiver is not "perfect" but is "good enough" in that the child only feels slight frustration.

Winnicott's gift to parents is that "good enough" is just that. Failure and disappointment by the mother or father are inevitable. What the child learns in this process of give and take is that "good enough" is dependable and sure. Most parents, more often the mother, suffer for their imperfection as a loving parent. If the mother's complete adaptation to the baby's need goes on too long, and does not decrease naturally, the baby's growing sense of a real external world apart from himself or herself is interrupted. The infant lingers in the magical world of illusion and hallucination. That is, the infant believes that simply having a need will lead to its immediate fulfillment. This, says Winnicott, is an illusion—although a necessary illusion. If the baby does not feel these minor amounts of frustration, she or he will not form a concept of external reality. Winnicott emphasizes that the earlier phase of mothering is equally essential for the baby's healthy development. But the ability to have an illusion is a necessary prerequisite to developing a sense of reality.

The concept of blessing for being is not a qualitative understanding of the long-suffering parent and the demanding infant. It goes beyond that, so the child's inner world is shaped and blessed at a different stage of formation by one who offers affirmation and love in moments when the child seeks to grow and risks their self-esteem in doing so. The blessing for being can be recognized by children as they understand at some deep level that they are loved.

This power of affirmation is closely linked with what Erikson and other developmentalists identify as the issue of trust/distrust. Children face big issues from birth forward. In their nearly total dependency, all their needs must be met by others—parents, layers of family members, and the proverbial community. Children, in turn, come to accept that their needs will be met, and this confidence is the foundation for life. How many of our early stories are built on this foundation of assurance? Or how do our stories highlight some insecurity, absence, or unmet need? Erik Erikson felt these specific needs in his own life and was forced to explore his own inadequate beginnings. He took note of the deficiencies and was forced to reimagine himself in order to live purposefully. All children need sufficient boundaries that are consistently established, even if that support falters on occasion, in order for them to move forward with a sense of confidence that the world they embrace will challenge them but will not crush their spirits.

One's inner child is encapsulated in memories of specific events or experiences. But no matter how old one may become, the inner child, like every other stage of life, is held within and can be grieved in shame or sorrow or celebrated in joy and remembrance. The vault of stories is important in that they allow one to move forward in time and growth and yet remain attached to the child within. Perhaps memory is a leaky vessel, but it is what we have. In truth, our inner world is populated by the many iterations of self: the adolescent, the young adult, and so on. The multiple forms of self that are held within help us hold together the library of memory. Adults often grieve the death of their inner child in some stagnant, freighted memory that relates to adult responsibility, serious endeavor, anxiety and cares, and bearing the burden of enormous promises that must be kept. Eventually, the loss can be identified at a stage where personal freedom can be claimed. Wearing purple hats with your friends or even living out some manic age-phobic reaction like taking up motorcycles can be different verses of the same song.

No matter how it manifests, there is usually a verdant period of life when this ancient childlikeness can be revived. Most go on a search for it in middle age or even as they move to retirement, when the shackles of responsible adulthood have been broken. The question is whether it's too little or too late, but something is better than nothing. We do what we can.

One early memory comes when I recall the happy occasions when Mom and Dad would place my little child body between their big adult bodies and hug me so fully that there was no part of me that was not being hugged. In that sublime family hug, I was caressed so completely that it almost squeezed the breath out of me, but I never felt anything but absolute love and acceptance. Love turned into giggles, which spilled over into joy.

I also have a strong sensory memory of the day I climbed up our neighbor's ladder that was leaning against his roof. I don't remember the neighbor who lived next door, but I do know I was beckoned by his ladder to explore a new world. Once on the roof, I stood at the peak and looked down over the elevated expanse of houses in our neighborhood, most of which formed the playgrounds of adventures shared with my friends. I remember sitting on the peak and being mesmerized by the way in which the neighborhood appeared different from above. I could see how the houses lined the street and how the streets around us were knitted together as a platted, intentional way of organizing the community where I lived—streets lined with houses, backyards surrounded by fences outlining and defining the play area or a space for the neighborhood dogs. Even the trees were somehow different, as I was seeing them from a height I could not have gained other than by climbing them. From above, it was a three-dimensional layout of houses, garages, and front and back yards instead of the two-dimensional flatlander's view I had on the ground. In a sense of great mystery, this was my first glimpse into the transcendence of an altered landscape. The only view of the world I had until that time was from ground level, and now I could see the world from overhead, from an elevated viewpoint, and everything about the way I saw the world changed.

As a child, my earliest stories were played out on the urban grid of three houses, each alongside the others with a street dividing two from one. The middle house was on one corner, and on the other corner was the third house. All three were inhabited by my maternal and paternal families, and each family member became a major actor in my earliest stories. My maternal grandparents lived across the street from my paternal grandmother. My mother's brother and sister-in-law and my sister-cousin lived in the house alongside that of my maternal grandparents. In my preschool days, my older brother and I were dropped off at our mother's mother's house while our parents worked. She watched over the two of us and our sister-cousin, who lived next door. While our four parents rushed off to their jobs, we three children likewise went to our work consisting of the day's adventures across the landscape of two adjoining homes and their backyards and across the street to another home and another yard, all a part of our full family tree where we were authorized as the youngest members to play and enjoy with no negative repercussions, as we had family rights to all three properties.

We lived as if we were the Little Rascals acting out whatever fancies we could sandwich into the daily regimen of prescribed naps and lunch and any snacks we could score. And there were the afternoon serial cowboy shows with their good guys and bad men on TV. There were also comedies, early sitcoms in which characters weathered a weekly crisis and offered lessons of morality and the struggle of doing the right thing. We were willing participants to the dawning age of television, and we spent time every afternoon on the floor watching the shows that are now seen as TV classics. In my mind, these three houses function like the set of a 1950s television drama. Our grandfather and uncle were television men who ran a TV and radio repair shop a few blocks away, so early on we always had a modest television. Since we were in a big city, we had four channels from which to choose. There were soap operas that we could not stand, but there was at least one channel with shows more to our liking or even a channel that had afternoon cartoons. We were television kids plopped down to see the regular rotation of Westerns and family shows that starred the pioneering comics of the 1950s. In looking back, this three-house dramatic stage was where we lived out many of our childhood memories. We moved seamlessly from the afternoon TV shows to our personal stories that we acted out as though we had our own show in which we were the stars. We ran in and out through gates from one yard to another. Occasionally we drifted across the street to our paternal grandmother's yard and sat on her porch while she was at work. We felt fully authorized to do this by our father's mother because we were her treasured grandchildren. We watched TV together. We played imaginative games together. On occasion, we would wrestle and call it fighting. If it got too quiet, one of us would yell, "Let's fight!" just before leaping onto the closest person. No one was upset with anyone, and wrestling was a primal way of showing love to the others. We napped together and ate our meals and snacks together, so why wouldn't we fight each other?

Our grandmother was the prosecuting attorney, judge, and jury—all in one—an all-powerful person whom we respected and adored and feared. She kept a chicken pen in the backyard from which we learned to find the eggs that had been laid and bring them into the kitchen. But we also learned one of our first hardships in life. Two working men would come home for lunch and there were three of us grandchildren, so every now and then, she would cull a chicken from the yard and kill it for our lunch. I remember this happening on several occasions and marveled at the bloody death that provided such a scrumptious meal. She had her own method for killing, not the usual neck wringing many describe. Instead, she would take a board just wide enough to cover the chicken's scrawny neck, hold the body in place with her clunky grandma shoes standing on the ends of the board, then reach down and pick up the helpless chicken by the legs and, with one quick jerk, sever the head from the body, which was released to flop convulsively around the yard. To our shock and horror but also to our strange sense of pleasure, it left a bloody trail as it flailed all over the yard willy-nilly. The three of us agreed that a woman who killed so easily was a woman to be feared.

But how did the arrangement of these houses reflect a life that predated my own? What prologue stories were being shaped that welcomed me to join the stories already in motion? Everyone I've mentioned was already in place, living out their own stories, when I joined the drama. Their stories were told and retold around the table at meals and in the backyard at dusk while we chased lightning bugs and our parents and grandparents sat in lawn chairs sipping sweet iced tea.

The TV and radio repair shop run by our grandfather and uncle was just a few blocks away, and so promptly at noon they would come home for lunch and to smoke a few cigarettes in the living room before going back for the afternoon's work. All of this went on for several years until our sister-cousin went off to first grade, followed the next year by my older brother, and I was left alone with my grandmother. The vault of shared stories is drawn from the experiences of being together with such familiar regularity. Oddly, almost no stories have survived of the year I spent alone with my grandmother waiting for my own turn at first grade.

At the end of the day, our parents would pick us up and take us home. We lived freely and seamlessly in the two worlds of our nuclear and extended families. Those early experiences do not overshadow my experience in my own family in the suburban home where I lived with my brother and with our mother and father. Rather, those three houses were vital extensions of the home that welcomed me at my birth. Those homes were each supportive of the other. Life under my grandmother's care undergirded everything I knew at home with my parents. They were different experiences by and large, but they were so consistent as to be, in my thinking, a seamless nest.

Looking over my shoulder and reflecting on this time, I see that as a child I was immersed in knowing four generations of people in my mother's family and three generations in my father's family. I understood them as important characters in comprehending my own life and in grasping the lingering influence of the generation that preceded my oldest family members. Those stories embraced me and were a part of the inherited narrative of my family.

In wanting to explore the stories of others so you can explore and understand your own stories, there's an old generational technique that says, "Talk to the oldest person in your family tree and ask them to tell you about the oldest family member they remember." When I first became a pastor, one of my parishioners shook my hand and told me I had now shaken hands with someone who had shaken hands with someone who had shaken Abraham Lincoln's hand. Not only that, he said, but I had now shaken hands with someone who shook the hand of someone who had shaken hands with a man who had shaken George Washington's hand. You may need to draw these connections on a piece of paper to fully comprehend their meaning. Even our personal touch reaches across time. Add it up in the past. Now think of how your personal touch will also reach across the span of time as a past and future reach that will astound you.

Gordon Cosby died in his nineties. He was the founding pastor of the Church of the Savior in Washington, D.C. When Pastor Cosby was asked to speak to a group of children, he thought about what he might tell them. Children are painfully literal in their thinking and don't tolerate an adult telling them something "not quite truthful"; most kids are brighter than we give them credit for being, and they resent anyone who speaks condescendingly to them.

Knowing this, Reverend Cosby told them he had two truths to share with them that morning that might help them understand the path they would take from being children to becoming adults. "According to the Bible," he said, "life gets better and better as it goes along. That is, it really is better to be a child than an infant, better to be an adolescent than a child, better to be a young adult than an adolescent, better to be a middle-aged adult than a young adult, and so on." Then he added, "And life gets harder and harder as it goes along; that is, it is harder to be a child than an infant, harder to be an adolescent than a child, harder to be a young adult than an adolescent, and so on . . . ."[50]

Children are on the path toward an ever-expanding life in which they will eventually embrace their calling as well as a world of people they can't even imagine. Some of those people will be friends and lovers. Some will be colleagues and mentors. Others will either encourage them or oppose them in the directions they choose to take. Children can't see all these forces, but they can begin thinking now about how they will accept them. They are exploring their contract in life even if they are unaware of its content. Children have role models who are prepared to give them guidance and support and love. Their world will expand and grow, and they will learn their lessons in life as has every other person they will encounter.

Story Starters: Childhood

• **Birth stories.** Is there a special significance to your name? Where are you located in birth order in relationship to siblings, cousins, and other extended family members? What was the family narrative at your birth? Are there any ongoing stories or themes? How did your family make room for you? What rituals were observed at your birth?

• **Expectations at your birth.** It's hard to believe there might have been anything but goodness and light at your long-expected arrival, but have you come to understand how your birth was celebrated or how it was a struggle for your family? What expectations, spoken and unspoken, were placed on you? What disappointments were identified with your birth?

• **Bedtime.** What habits of going to sleep and waking up do you remember? What made those moments important? What bedtime habits do you keep, even today?

• **Name.** What story can you tell about your name? How did you receive your name? Did your parents plan for your name, or did they come up with it at your birth? What stories do you know about it? Does your name have significance or represent someone in your family, perhaps someone you're named after? Does your name align with some cultural background?

• **Birthdays.** How did your family celebrate your birthday? Where do you fit in the birth order? What difference did it make? Did gender make a difference?

• **Christmas.** What Christmas memories from childhood have you carried over into your adult life?

• **Love/Comfort.** Was there a tangible way in which you experienced peace, love, and comfort? Was there a time when you wanted love, comfort, or peace but did not receive it? Who made the feeling of love or comfort real to you?

• **Fear.** Did you have a special fear as a child? What was it? How did you handle your fear? Is that fear still powerful for you today?

• **Abandonment.** Abandonment stories are often called "lost" stories, as they recall a time when you were lost or separated from your family. When did you first experience aloneness? How did your parents react upon finding you? How did you feel when you were found? Was your relocation made special in some way?

• **Meals.** What special food or meal do you remember? What special meaning did it have or signify?

• **God/Faith.** How is faith present in your stories? How is faith present in the lives of the people you encountered at your birth? Is there a faith tradition you have joined? Is it still present in your life now? What God stories can be told from these traditions?

• **Preparing for Essay Five.** Recall your stories of adolescence and select a category from the questions suggested at the end of the next session (see p. 95–97). If you are part of a group study, come ready with a story to explore!

Journal

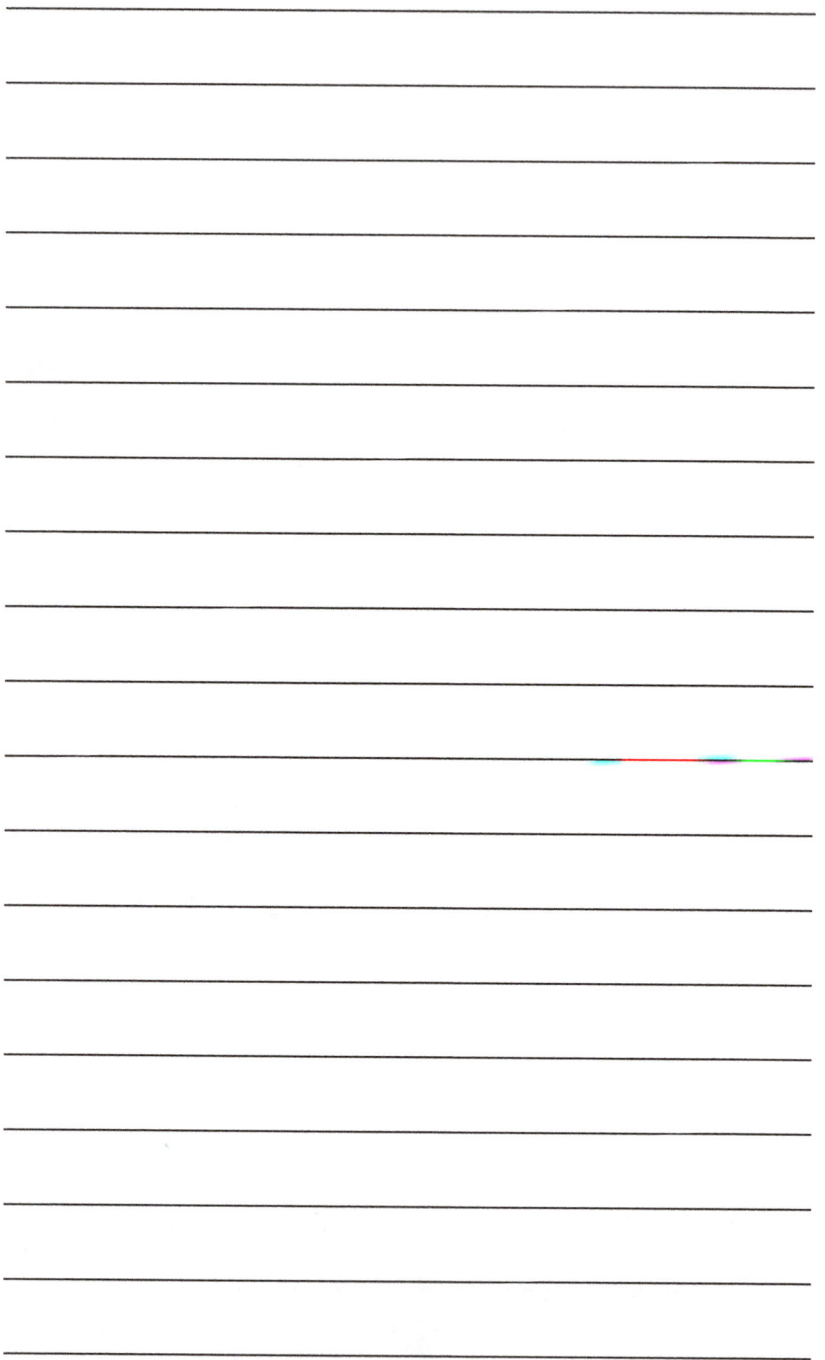

Adolescence–
The Second Decade

I am the one who very nearly perfected the art and beauty of being a child, but then, out of nowhere, things changed. Everything came unglued, and changes were set loose in body, emotions, hormones, and social relationships. One year I was fully at home in my body, self-aware, cool and confident in thought and place in the world, and the next year I was a stumbling, bumbling mess. I am the one who crashed across the threshold separating childhood from adolescence.

I am insecure as I stumble into a different dimension with new rules. My body is changing in ways that make me self-conscious and uncomfortable. I have to figure out new routines of hygiene, and I'm not used to this unfamiliar body I inhabit. How do I navigate the changes in my thoughts and emotions? I am unsteady about my ungainly life, how I look, how I talk, how I feel, how I dress. How long can one person keep this charade up? Who am I?

I'm mesmerized by a new world with nuances I can juggle as I am able to see what I couldn't see before. My self-conscious thoughts are a burden, and I obsess about insecurities at more levels than I can manage. I become moody and mercurial even as I become reclusive. I can explode in anger or implode in self-doubt. I'm defensive about both my behavior and my motives. I tire of all the intrusive and controlling questions from my parents, my siblings and friends, and my teachers. Adults are generally a pain in the backside with all their demands, expecting me to respond to every comment, every inquiry, all the mindless chatter about who cares what. I am the one whose inner life has blossomed and withered in equivalence to the fluctuations in my outer life, and the vibrant growth in my inner life can quickly turn arid and empty like a desert. I am highly self-critical about how I look, how I talk, and how I act. I'm more aware of my endless inner monologues, neurotic conversations scripted by some nihilist. I don't give myself a break on anything and can mercilessly pulverize any possibility of hope.

Sex, love, and intimacy are the new frontiers. I am obsessed with furtive thoughts about things I can't fully imagine. I'm irresistibly drawn, but to what? I don't even know, but I'm dying to find out. In some deep mystery, I want to possess someone and I want to be possessed in equal measure. I don't know it yet, but I want an intimacy so beyond anything I have ever known, completely absorbed by another, something at once pure and overwhelming, yet something for the shadows. Add to this the fact that I'm drawn to the dream of romantic love. Does such a thing exist? All of this is beyond my knowing, a perfect blend of physical, emotional, and soul-ish. Practice rounds of intense intimacy and the search for love are messy experiences. In truth, I know almost nothing of substance, but I am mesmerized and want to know what I do not yet know. Both opposite-gender and same-gender relationships are loaded with new meaning and curiosities, and I am simultaneously at war and best friends with my peers.

Everything becomes complicated in this new world. I have questions, big questions, but no one of whom I can ask them. All these changes produce anxiety about my place in the world. To compound matters, I live on a social battlefield where the "innies" rule over the "outies," leaving the rest of us in a crowded middle ground, a no-man's land of social struggle. I obsess about my place in the world and build fragile alliances to give me a sense of safety and assurances that do not hold. I'm beginning to shape a personal way of being, but this is not the result of a reasoned study; it's more like a timely social experiment built on success and failure.

I can tell a lie to cover my tracks, the bigger the better, but my lies have a diminishing effectiveness as they seldom hold steady in the searing light of day. I've told lies about others to hurt them. I've bent the rules, broken the rules, and made a mess of me. These are practice rounds, and what I'm trying to calibrate is how to make my inner world line up with my outer world. At times I'm like a lost child trying to find my way home.

My thought life is deepening as I'm able to enjoy adult-like thoughts. I can now see what I could not see before: the world of abstractions. Before I could only see unvarnished literalism. I can do complicated math problems. I can experience science as a view of the world from both the microscope and the telescope. I can juggle moral dilemmas to recognize that there is more than right and wrong and the black and white of my childhood. I can hold two opposing thoughts, seeking equilibrium of truth as moral polarities consisting of and including various shades of gray. I've learned to love irony and upside-down, contradictory humor. Satire is my new best friend.

I am also able to have a deep awareness of that which is larger than me and to sense the presence of a divine mystery we might call God. There is a world religion zoo out there, and I'm unsettled by the fact that my religion is not the only show in town. I assume my family has guided me toward our religion, but other families at least as religious as mine hold altogether different religious truths. Does God live in everyone's house of faith? Are metaphors the language of the mystery of the divine, beyond comprehension, beyond words, beyond the images themselves until we come to see God as metaphorical puff for that which cannot be fully seen, fully known, fully experienced? I am working my way to a deeper understanding of myself as I come to accept myself as a person, immersed into the family of others but also unique and of value.

❧

When Erik Erikson wrote about this age, he followed the issue of childhood trust with the growing sense of self-control that's at the heart of adolescence. He wrote that those of this age are driven by the conflict between autonomy and shame/doubt. Many confuse autonomy with individualism, while it appears that Erikson was more focused on the concept of autonomy in contrast to heteronomy. Autonomy in Erikson's view is about "functioning independently without control of others," meaning one is self-governing or relying on oneself or one's abilities. This stands in contradiction to heteronomy, or how one is controlled by others.[51] Erikson implied that self-governing is a natural extension of the issue of trust first faced in childhood. The distinctions are slight but important. A child certainly embraces trust in another but also faces trust in oneself as a form of self-trustworthiness by living in "a widening social radius."[52] This basis in trust creates a platform on which the child may widen their sense of relating incrementally with others and with oneself and thereby living a larger life. In the counterweight to trust, an adolescent will face shame and doubt. Shame is a painful feeling of having lost the respect of others due to improper behavior or incompetence, either by oneself or by someone who is closely associated. Doubt may follow shame based on one's poor behavior or living below one's best self.

In our consideration of the arc of life, I am following the writings of Donald Capps, who breaks the arc of life from birth to death into five somewhat indistinct periods and attaches to these stages a decadal framework (childhood, adolescence, young adulthood, middle adulthood, and older adulthood). I use the term "indistinct" with intent, as each stage overlaps the one before and the one after. For example, while most assume that adolescence ends at the beginning of one's twenties, some consider it as extending into the late twenties, which would make this stage inclusive of the second and third decades. But others consider young adulthood to consume also the third and fourth decades. The overlap is obvious. The same argument could be waged about the line separating young adulthood from middle adulthood, or from middle adulthood to older adulthood. The truth is, there are no distinct lines. We wake up one day and realize we've crossed a border, and from that day forward we lean into the next stage and may be nostalgic about the stage we've left or perhaps grieve that we're growing markedly older.

The ongoing stages of the arc of life will be considered under the wisdom described by the nineteenth century Danish philosopher Søren Kierkegaard, who said, "Philosophy is perfectly right in saying that life must be understood backward. But then one forgets the other clause—that it must be lived forward."[53] If there are lines separating age stages from one to the next, everyone understands that we only cross them when we're ready. There are maturational markers, but surely it's more complicated than that. We mature physically, emotionally, intellectually, and in our willingness to deal with the appropriate life challenges in unique, individual ways. As mentioned, Capps reimagines Erikson's stages of life as decadal. In that structure, all of childhood from birth to preadolescence falls within the first decade of life. He ignores the Freudian early childhood stages of development, and for our purposes they are unnecessary as they are consumed with only the first year.

Within a decadal framework, the last of childhood is considered transitional or preparatory growth before the shift into adolescence in which critical growth toward maturity is encountered and embraced. Leaving childhood is the challenge, and the pull of adolescence in the same way becomes the challenge of young adulthood. Is it the push of the one or the pull of the other? In the years between childhood and young adulthood, one faces multiple growth fronts at once. There is nothing smooth and easy about navigating these waters. Paul wrote, "When I was a child, I spoke like a child, I thought like a child, I reasoned like a child; when I became an adult, I put an end to childish ways."[54] There's not a single event that marks this shift, and for most people, it is a slow, grinding, transitional process that occurs over months or years. This shift occurs in the second decade that begins in childhood and ends in young adulthood. Unbeknownst to us in focused awareness, we go through this second decade in search of ourselves. We are people in the making, on our way to somewhere, but where?

In either the fifth or sixth grades, my best friend at the time and I were in a dime store in our neighborhood. I have no idea why, but he and I decided we would wander around in the store and slipped items in our pockets. It felt like a game, a stupid game of "let's see if we can get away with this." The manager was sitting in an elevated half-office sentry above the aisles of merchandise in the store and was a good judge of our all-too-obvious actions. When we walked out of the store, he pulled us back inside, where he took us to the back room and asked us to empty our pockets. There was nothing of real value on the countertop, but it was store merchandise and our crime was undeniable. He threatened to call either the police or our parents. We both gave him our home phone numbers, and he called our parents, announcing that they could come and pick us up.

The shame was immediate. I don't know what happened at my friend's house, but I clearly remember what happened at mine. It was late afternoon by the time I got home, and both my mother and my father called a meeting for the three of us to sit down and talk about what I had done. I remember my mother crying. Both were clinical in their assessment of the event and reminded me that I was not raised in a home where this kind of behavior was allowed. I was reminded that I was a Boy Scout who had pledged myself as one who would follow the Boy Scout Oath, which prescribes certain aspects of character I had clearly ignored. I don't recall an appeal to my religious beliefs because this would not be the approach my nonreligious father would have taken. I probably felt that level of guilt in my own heart, and all of the approaches used to bring me to my senses were equally effective in helping me confront the shame of what I had done. I had shamed my mother and father. Their child was now a criminal, a lowlife shoplifter. My last comment on this experience was that I was forced to come to grips with my own poor judgment. I was not the instigator, but I had foolishly followed my friend's lead in stealing and consequently experienced a deep sense of shame. This was absorbed by my parents as one of those ugly episodes in which I learned a hard lesson in life about giving away my autonomy.

The passage from childhood through adolescence to young adulthood is awkward at times, occasionally perilous, and filled with fractured memories of battles waged, battles won, and battles lost. In emotional terms, it was like learning to walk again. The feeling of equilibrium is seldom experienced with confidence or assurance. This is also a time of disruption in the parent-child bond as the adolescent must learn to separate from the parents in order to follow their own path. Parents must allow enough flexibility in order to recognize that this is ultimately a healthy process, a necessary step to be taken in order for the child to become a self-guided, healthy adult. There is pain as the adolescent takes a healthy step forward but also awkwardly takes a painful step away in the relationship. Most of this is not discussed, only acted out between parents and child.

Erikson was no stranger to the challenge for both parents and child in this awkward tango of relationship with autonomy and heteronomy. In this second decade, the child struggles with the tension between "cooperation and willfulness" and "the freedom of self-expression and its suppression."[55] The challenge for parents is to guide their child to find self-control without sacrificing self-esteem. The hoped-for result is a lasting sense of autonomy in which one has the tools to move through life with a sense of direction and assurance. In parenting, the issue is identifiable: too much or too little? Too much suppression creates impotence, loss of self-control, and parental over-control that leaves the child with a lasting sense of doubt and shame.[56] The goal is to find a balance that includes firmness and support and enough wiggle room for the adolescent to know what it is like to hold the reins of their life. Children in the second decade of adolescence need the right balance to move with confidence through this decade and on to adulthood and self-sufficiency.

Like many, my most painful memories come from the early stages of adolescence, when I was clearly no longer a child but not skilled at the more mature years of being a teenager. In this time, I remember feeling in a foul mood at least as much as I felt good. My foul mood was chiefly related to how I felt insecure about myself. I was nervous and worried, and anxiety seemed to be my baseline emotional state. I had shifted from being a happy child to being an angry young teenager. In fact, if queried, I doubt I could have put words to my feelings; I seemed to be the last one to observe my own emotional state with clarity. In this stage, I could not regulate my moods if I could not name them. I could feel my feelings with great drama, but I could not describe them with any certainty. My body had grown more quickly than my emotions or my self-reflection. I was too big to be a child but so out of balance with myself as to be living in some twilight zone as a person. Crossing this liminal threshold did not happen overnight but was drawn across months and years of painful growth.

In this time, I remember I did something (I don't remember what) to upset my mother, who turned to grab me in order to spank me. Spanking was no real threat, mind you, nor was it painful. I saw her pivot in my direction (I knew this move from past experience), and before she could take a step closer, I took a step in her direction. No words were said that I recall, but my move was a direct challenge to her that we were no longer to relate to one another in a way in which a spanking would be tolerated. I'm sure my move toward her was assertive enough to give her sober pause about what to do next. I was the child who needed spanking, as opposed to my older brother, whom I don't recall needing them. Being unable to punish me by spanking gave my mother new weapons. She now sat me down to talk to me, a punishment harsher than any beating she could have applied. Together on this day of correction, we both crossed into new territory. Looking back, I should have let her spank me for a while longer, as she perfected a mode of conversation that continued well into my young adulthood in those moments when she wanted to continue to parent me. These are the steps toward separation that we all must navigate if we're to move toward independence. The maps we follow are known in the literature about parent and child, but at the time we are navigating the territory, those maps are confounding, something we can only recognize in later reflection or when we become the parents of our own children and find ourselves in the same old territory but in a different role. At the point where self-awareness is most needed, most of us at this age do not possess the ability to think outside of ourselves for understanding or validation.

What I recognize now is that my parents were also navigating their own roles in our relationship. As I've already noted, being my older brother's parent was a different challenge than being my parent. We were different due to our birth order and to our way of managing our lives. I can see now what I couldn't really see then—that both of our parents were working hard to provide what we needed as a family and that they bore great stress during this time. My father had broken away from a low-paying, nominal job in a printing press to open his own business as a commercial artist. That was a bold move that drove him out of his comfort zone to be assertive in meeting people, knocking on doors, and becoming more of a salesman than his quiet, thoughtful personality would normally allow. My mother was a secretary for a family-run insurance company. She worked throughout our childhood with the support of her mother, who kept us when we were preschoolers. A decade after my older brother was born, our mother gave birth to our younger brother, and she quit working so she could stay home to raise him. At this time, we bought a new home as the smaller, post-WWII home was now inadequate for our needs. My father's business must have become more reliable, although I still remember these as "the lean years." How did my parents do it? I have no idea.

Being the parents of two boys who were now moving into adolescence along with a newborn infant was a challenge for my parents in balancing how they loved us and in continuing to help us grow appropriately. We were involved in church activities (with the exception of my father), scouting, and other activities related to school such as band and athletics. The social life for the family centered on these groups with whom we held many things in common and with the extended families of my father and mother. I remember a few family vacations and occasional family camp-outs that, much later, included their grandchildren.

It is widely understood that anyone younger than twenty is not yet an adult, even though they are capable of doing adult things. For many reasons, they are considered children. For a period of time, they are "tweeners." Many developmental psychologists believe adolescence is still descriptive emotionally, intellectually, and physically into one's twenties—all growth fronts that are moving toward maturity. Similarly, where is the line in childhood that separates the child from adolescence? These are the gray zones that the legal system answers one way and psychologists and parents answer another way. Adolescent peers scoff at it all and claim to hold the authoritative answer based on their inner wisdom.

Generally speaking, the path forward for girls can be substantively different than for boys. Many girls, upon puberty, leave behind their brave explorer world and go quiet, their inner selves outwardly voiceless and unsure. Psychotherapist Mary Pipher says, "Girls become fragmented, their selves split into mysterious contradictions. They are sensitive and tenderhearted, mean and competitive, superficial and idealistic."[57] Boys have similar battles to face, but with vastly different tools. Many face their insecurities through competition in sports and academics, although this is also true for many girls. Boys may work out the pecking order in life through the externals of these activities rather than in the dark hallways of their minds.

The possibility of being lost is a part of our journey toward maturity. Being lost and being found are metaphors for our experience at this age. Being lost can hit any of us at almost any time, but perhaps more certainly when we move from childhood to adolescence. It is as true for boys as it is for girls. In a powerful metaphor, Stevie Smith describes a man, lifeless upon a beach, who insists to witnesses, "I was much further out than you thought / And not waving but drowning."[58] Pipher acknowledges that teenagers often distance themselves from their parents just at the time when they most need their parents' support. As Smith points out, we don't always recognize others' struggles or their distance from help.

Both boys and girls are subject to a split in their inner selves—the split between the true self and the false self. This split is enough to be considered a dark journey through the wasteland of childhood and adolescence that takes place before the arrival in what we would call young adulthood. It is a pathway fraught with dangers, expansive on one front and imploding on other fronts. This is a season of storms that everyone must go through. There are no shortcuts, and there are no real solutions that protect adolescents from these storms. The ideal is for the significant people who have access to them to ensure that love is generously offered, acceptance is given in place of shame, and ample stores of patience are available for the length and breadth of this season. These are hatchlings who are forced to peck their way out of their shells, and those who don't find the energy to peck may die in those same shells. What else can be shared with them? We can give them a wide berth, but we should not abandon them in their season of need. Adulthood is achieved by traversing a land of demons, obstacles, and fractured thinking. While there are great moments of growth and exploration, this land can be savage and despairing. Some don't make it, and no one makes it through to the other side unmarked.

This quiet revolution is likely the cause of many unseen factors: eating disorders, drug and alcohol use, post-traumatic stress disorder from sexual assaults, sexually transmitted diseases, self-inflicted injuries, and rampant thoughts of suicide, not to mention the prevalence of adolescent depression and anxiety. The numbers of children in therapy have skyrocketed, and the use of prescribed medications has likewise risen dramatically. Children today come from homes split by divorce, suffer from alcoholism and drug use, and explore casual sex at early ages. Many adolescents live in a wasteland littered with despair and emptiness.

Columnist Clarence Page identifies the "electronic wallpaper" of media that does a poor job of educating adolescents in this shadowy existence. This wallpaper distracts children from focusing on the issues at hand and causes them to drift through this stage without attending to the growth challenges that they should solve. Interestingly, Mary Pipher doesn't blame dysfunctional parenting; instead, she blames a pervasive dysfunctional culture that has more influence on our children than we do. She identifies four coping strategies that adolescents use to protect themselves. They (1) conform, (2) withdraw, (3) become depressed, or (4) get angry.[59] These aren't strategies; they are defensive weapons of war. These aren't strategies to win; they are efforts merely to survive. The world has gotten coarser and meaner and more sexualized than ever. Our children on the path to adulthood struggle mightily to get from one daunting challenge to another.

Our work for this stage of life is to find our way forward toward a calling, a purpose. Poet and essayist Wendell Berry offers a simple insight about our goal during this period: "Find something that needs doing and do it."[60] We grow toward fulfillment, each in our own way, and often we discover our direction, the life we are meant to live, as we follow the daily invitations to life. This map is not foreordained but is discovered as we live our lives. In that dynamic challenge, there are discoveries, "aha" moments of clarity, that reach out to us to guide us to unknown shores. Through these happenstance occurrences, we may find ourselves drawn in a new direction.

What drives our need to *become*? In what ways can we suggest that we are formed all across the arc of our lives "to make ourselves useful," as novelist John Irving suggests?[61] James Hillman, Jungian psychologist, poses a thesis about the power of innate motivation to describe how we are guided toward a purpose in life, how we find that purpose, or how we are drawn into a search for the thing the motivation is moving us to discover about our life's mission. To illustrate this motivation, he draws from the relationship between the acorn and oak, wondering, "Is not psychology's 'motivation' the push in the acorn of the oak—or, better, the oakness of the acorn? Oaks bear acorns, but acorns are pregnant with oaks."[62] Everyone needs a guiding thought, a central theme that seems to mark the boundaries around their world so they can understand it. Hillman claims, "Each life is formed by its unique image, an image that is the essence of that life and calls it to a destiny. As the force of fate, this image acts as a personal *daimon*,[63] an accompanying guide who remembers your calling. . . . Each person enters the world called." The acorn theory is thus "about calling, about fate, about character, about innate image." How do we know this? How does this idea feel right? It comes from "reading life backward." Reading life backward means that "the innate image of your fate holds all in the interconnected presence of today, yesterday, and tomorrow. Your person is not a process or a development. You are that essential image that develops, if it does. As Picasso said, 'I don't develop; I am.'" Hillman's Acorn Theory is useful in that it helps answer the questions, how do I put together into a coherent image the pieces of my life? How do I find the basic plot of my story?

This is not an observation about determinism but an observation that we move from moment to moment or, more accurately, from choice to choice, connecting the dots to create a map of our journeys. In other words, we choose our way to a future we create by narrowing the range of options through our choices. These include the intentional choices and the choices that are not intentional in the usual sense but are made nevertheless. Futurists describe a "futures tree" that illustrates how this works. A futures tree recognizes the value of each decision that extends the direction we take in creating the map we follow in life. Each decision has the power to carry our story down new pathways, as each simple response to life has future implications. In this understanding, all of life is engaged. Each step taken is embedded with possibilities for the future, even including the events we might call tragic or disastrous. In this view, everything is useful. All results have the power to change the trajectory of life in new and unexpected directions. The map has all the elements of an unknown country, but it is a path we can see from beginning to end.

Story Starters: Adolescence

• **Leftovers from Childhood.** Every age stage with the exception of childhood will consider which issues from the previous stage continue into the next. For example, what habits of childhood do you continue, perhaps even to this day? What habits or rituals from childhood remain meaningful in your life as an adolescent?

• **Family.** Who was the most important family member to you apart from your parents? Did you make a ritual with this person that signified their importance? How did your family ritualize their own existence? What practice made your family come to life and helped you realize you were not only included but also vitally important?

• **Social Life.** What helped you expand your life beyond the family home when you began to spend less time there and more time away?

• **Friends.** What rituals did you adopt that signified you were no longer a child? How did you and your friends share a ritual that signified you were no longer children and were now adolescents (some ritual not shared or initiated by adults)?

• **Fear and Anxiety.** Most teens are anxious, perhaps even highly anxious. Did you have a special fear as an adolescent? What was it? How did you handle your fear? Is that fear still powerful for you? If not, how did things change to lessen that anxiety or fear?

• **Death.** Many adolescents face their first experience with death during this period. When did you first experience grief? Was it the death of a family member or friend? Was it the death of a pet? How did you first experience death and grief? What do you recall of how it was ritualized? Do you remember the first time you experienced death in your family? Who was it? How old were you? What do you remember?

• **God.** As a child, how did you understand God? How did the family or faith community help you understand God? What rituals did you observe that helped you experience God? How did you feel about that practice?

• **Forgiveness and Reconciliation.** Is there a story of pain or of wrong that runs through your stories? If so, how did you come to experience it? Did you know what it was like to be understood, to be accepted, despite something grievous you did or suffered? Did you come to a point at which someone of importance forgave you or sought your forgiveness?

• **Love/Romance/Sexuality.** For most, this is the stage of life when love and romance are significantly experienced for the first time. First love, first touch, first kiss, first . . . . How did your family and/or friends mark this moment in your life? How did you handle rejected love?

• **Driving a Car.** When you passed your driving test, whose car did you drive? How did you get your first car? Did you pay for it or was it provided? Most kids hit a speed bump after obtaining this new freedom (pun intended), whether with a driving violation, a wreck, or some other mishap. If this happened to you, how did your parents handle it? What happened?

• **Spending Money.** How did your family handle your increased needs for money to pay for your activities? What did you contribute, and how did you earn your money? How did you and your family talk about money?

• **Education.** If you went to college (university, community college, specialized training) after high school, how was the decision made? How did you decide what to study? How did you decide to stay at home or to go away for school? What expectations did your family share with you? What expectations did you express to them?

• **Maturity.** When did you first realize you were no longer a child and were now a teenager? What signs of maturity did you demonstrate to signify this? Likewise, what signs of maturity showed that you were ready for young adulthood? Did you and your family celebrate these achievements in any way?

• **Preparing for Essay Six.** If you are part of a group, recall your stories of young adulthood and select a category from the questions suggested at the end of the next session. Come ready with a story to explore!

Journal

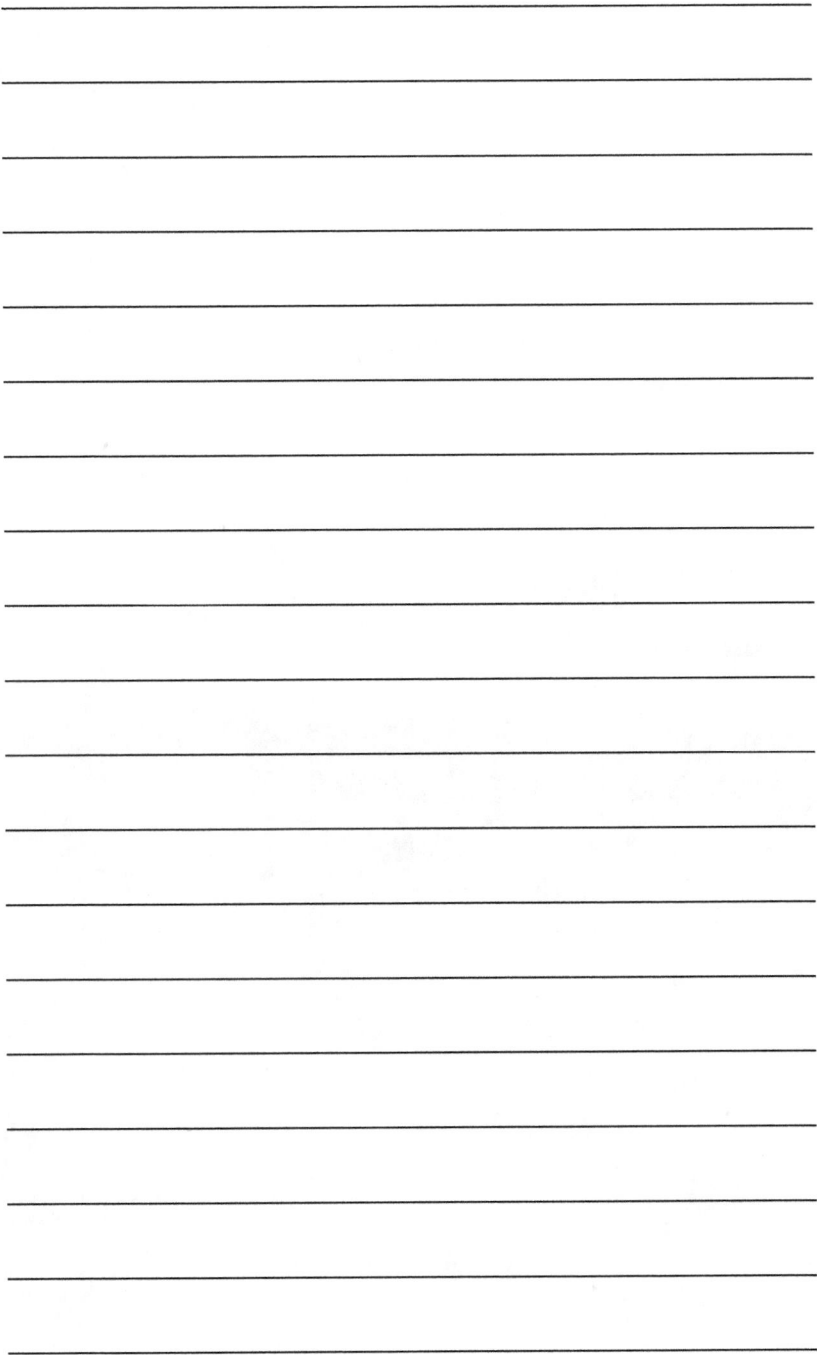

Young Adulthood– The Third and Fourth Decades

I am the one at yet another crossroads, only this time the stakes are higher and the degree of difficulty is greater. I am living in the betwixt and between, no longer this and not quite that. I can be serious-minded and dutiful, capable of critical thinking and dedicated to making my mark in the world. But I can also be silly, thoughtless, and irresponsible. I can make mistakes beyond my ability to assume responsibility. The wise old therapist cautions, "Make as many good decisions as you can in a row," and off we go on the path littered with our many decisions.

I am at the peak of my physical capabilities. I'm as athletic as I'll ever be. I'm in as good a physical shape as I'll ever be. My body will slowly crest the hill of adolescent development with the weight of time and physical maturity, and slowly I will become more sedentary from watching too much TV and ceasing physical activity. My body will succumb to its own decline. For most of us, "This is as good as it gets."

I may not be sitting in school, but I'm definitely still learning. I read what I can, but my learning may just as well be animated by a digital and visual world. I may be one who keeps plugging along in college, graduate school, or specialized training, and, if so, I may become an accomplished learner who excels in critical thinking and is adept at problem-solving. Under the right employment opportunities, if my personal or interpersonal issues don't hijack my future, I will be a success. The level of my success has the power to save me from an economic world that's underfunded and overspent.

I am working hard to figure out how life happens, as I'm no longer living under the tent of someone else's making. It's true that I'm living longer at home with my parents, but I may also be out on my own before I'm really equipped to manage my life. "Launching" may be a concern for my parents and friends, and I may make the same beginning steps over and over and over again. Why are things so hard? Finding my way is like a puzzle. The parts are all there, I suppose, but the opening moves are not. I suppose it would help if I was clair-voyant and could see over the horizon—to see a direction in life, to know who I am and what I am to be. It's hard to take a trail when I can't find the trail-head. No one tells me what to look for; the clues are all there, but I'm unable to recognize them. Could it be that everyone but me knows how my puzzle should be solved?

I wish I felt surer of myself. I feel every feeling and know so little of why I feel them when I do. There are times when I'm self-aware and pleased with myself and with my life. But there are also the dark times when I don't know who I am or why I exist. I can be moody and punishing of my inner world and even harder on my outer world. I am living in a world with no maps to orient me to what is normal or bizarre.

I am living in an age of many things. The world my eyes see is like a mirage, shimmering just beyond my fingertips. I am swamped with a world of possessions beyond my ability to acquire. Everything my eyes see lights up a level of desire I can't justify. My desires are an unquenchable thirst that my place in the world cannot support. Like most of my peers, I have more debts than assets. I owe for school, for the phone plan I'm using, for my digital toys and gadgets, for my car, and for my expensive "spend first" habits. I'm maxed out and redlining. Especially if I'm underpaid or struggling with medical bills, capping expenses is not in my grasp. I shop for little at the grocery store beyond the freezer section of precooked foods and the deli and don't have an at-home meal plan other than "going out." Savings? Rainy-day funds? I'm buried in the needs of the now, under the burden of more expenses than income, and have no plan to fund tomorrow. I'm juggling it all and praying to God that it doesn't fall down around me.

I am young and beautiful and don't even know it. I am talented and smart and good, but I am painfully insecure and neurotically self-critical. My eyes take in only the most egregious, dismissive view of myself. I have forgiveness and grace for everyone around me but have little for myself. I am a heat-seeking missile hoping to gather experience, adventure, wisdom, and fulfillment. I want my life to matter, and I want to give myself to commitments that only the pure in heart can tackle. My limited life experience gives my view of the world a rosy tint tinged with naïveté, but what perspective can I take other than the only one I have? Lord, have mercy.

Many of the big questions still loom ahead. Who am I? What is my purpose in life? What am I capable of doing and why? Whom will I love? Who will love me in return? What paths will I take in life? Can I succeed in life, or will failure uncover my inner fears of whether I have what it takes? This is the decade of big questions, and it demands a response that will shape the direction of my life. As I pursue answers, I will be establishing the trajectories of most of the important issues that will make my future life a reality.

I have convictions about right and wrong, about up and down, about left and right, and about here and there. I can tell the difference even though I can't always think clearly about what to do about it. I have a strong desire to see justice flourish, even though I'm only beginning to make my own life reflect my deepest inner convictions. I want my life to matter and I want to be strong in the right ways. I may be idealistic, but I cannot withhold my heart from feeling the way it does and for wanting to lay hold of the truth even if it's only in this one thing.

My political views are global and local but not driven by old party loyalties. I'm not a joiner unless we're talking about a gym or a club. I find myself on a merry-go-round, riding the same circuit over and over again in repetitive boredom. I get up and go to work. I work hard at a job that may be a form of slow death. I watch my favorite shows to soothe my frazzled nerves, shower, and hit the sack only to start again when the alarm goes off in the morning. I live on the set of Groundhog Day with next to no insight about what has happened to me. One day I walked across the stage to receive my diploma, and now I find myself lost in the woods with no map, no flashlight, and no provisions for the inevitable boredom of my life.

While I'm often alone, I also run in packs with my friends. We hang out and talk passionately, and when we're ginning, we are altogether entertaining to ourselves. We die laughing together. On occasion we are morose. We can drink inordinate amounts of alcohol and can cuss a blue streak with no shame or conscience. We're constantly on the prowl for intimacy, but too often we settle for sex alone. We can attach to another person with devotion or make serial connections with surprising frequency. There's the feeling that there is a window of opportunity guiding our romantic possibilities that may be open for now but could close with almost no warning, as though we're playing musical chairs with a panicky sense of despair. I'm dancing as fast as I can.

If I'm in a relationship, there's the possibility we will couple and make a bite-sized version of the two of us. Or maybe we decide to adopt. No matter, as now we have to renegotiate everything. Who's handling which chores and which responsibilities? We renegotiate how we relate to our friends and our families. We renegotiate our money and our needs in light of the needs of a third member of our family. We renegotiate our priorities and our values and our aspirations. We are standing on the shoreline of the sea and cannot see over the horizon to the distant land of the future. There's mostly only now.

I am the one who ponders the spirit that permeates the universe. Maybe God has a name, maybe not. God is not the God who lives at church. Many discover something about the mystery of God in churches that look like the set of a late-night show. Hipster preachers, slick bands, and swaying worshipers are the church of the Holy Vibe. It's not everyone's cup of tea, but neither is it your grandma's church. These kinds of churches are lubricated by coffee or beer and serving the world's needs with amazing compassion. God is found in the needs of the world, not in the folding chairs following the program.

⌘

This stage completes the first half of life. If one accepts an ancient norm for a whole life as "three score and ten" (Ps 90:10, KJV), this stage of young adulthood builds to a midpoint crescendo. One could easily not know they have begun this stage and may not realize they have left it for the middle stage of adulthood. In this first stage of adulthood, the lines are drawn loosely. It is murky leaving adolescence and even murkier crossing the midpoint of life.

What markers help us imagine this stage of young adulthood? Here's a sample list: leaving home, establishing values, enduring stress, nurturing affirmation of self, finishing education, landing a job, balancing friendships, having sex, building a family (or not), enriching life through spirituality, surviving failure, handling debt, discovering identity, enjoying mobility, befriending cynicism, and finding a balance in materialism. The markers of this age will vary widely. Some will experience a world of successes and acquisitions while others will falter, whether through circumstance or through poor choices. Some will find healthy, sustainable marriages; some will choose singleness; others will walk through the minefields of divorce and single parenthood. Welcome to the ambiguity of this first stage of adulthood!

Leaving home is a concept loaded with meaning. Leaving home should be understood as a part of the natural journey through adolescence toward independence/interdependence. It should mark our launch into the world of adulthood, apart from the care and keeping of our parents/family. Everyone finds their own way and establishes their own time frames.

Our preparation for work sharpens in focus and education becomes less fuzzy about its purpose. Our learning takes on new meaning as it is understood that our education will be connected to our ability to find meaningful work. The wish for meaningful work is tied to the understanding that we will successfully move away from home and make our way in the world. There are many who experience false starts as the reality of what it takes has been undeniably miscalculated. Moving back home is a hard-felt lesson in humility that raises questions about our resources and our ability to scheme a new world of self-reliance.

Most of us go through a series of seemingly meaningless jobs that are not considered anything more than a first plan to support ourselves. In 2017, McDonald's claimed to be "America's best first job." According to the company, McDonald's jobs are ideal for those who are new to the workforce due to the flexible schedule, nearby locations, and employee training programs. Working at McDonald's is a hands-on way to learn skills one will need in other, future career paths. Employees become skillful at teamwork by learning to work efficiently with other employees and solving problems as a group. One learns the people skills needed to keep customers happy, what it means to punch a clock, and what it's like to have taxes taken out of a paycheck. One learns what it means to be accountable to coworkers, managers, customers, and oneself. These are the lessons of the new wave of employees who are launching themselves into adulthood.

Not everyone works for McDonald's, but the task of learning how to work and how to find a meaningful expression of vocation is done in stages, one seemingly insignificant job after another as a long string of work experiences by which adolescents can find their own path. For many, this is the path of discovery through which they lay claim on whatever lays claim upon them. Jobs *du jour* are how we think about them. It is not considered out of the ordinary to move from one job to another over a relatively brief period of time. Hopefully, these jobs are means unto an end, helping us gather needed exposure to a wide variety of work that helps us figure out what we should do in life. These jobs teach us about responsibility and acceptance even when we don't want to learn those lessons. They become the gateway to understanding what is taught in high school as "Personal

Economics." These low-level jobs may lead us back to school. Or at least they may sharpen our goals for education.

In the transitory age when I was still in school and not launched on a career path, I had several different jobs. At age fifteen, I worked one blazing summer digging by hand the foundation of a new church mission for next to nothing per hour. I worked in two university libraries while in school. I delivered tropical fish to small stores in the North Texas region while also working in a dime store. I delivered mattresses to homes. I painted houses with a partner. I served as a teacher's aide in an elementary school where the only other man was the old custodian. As the only able-bodied man in the school, I broke up fights in the cafeteria and muscled a drug-addled sixth grade kid who was about as big as I was out of a third-floor window. I drove a school bus for a nearby school district morning and afternoon. I worked one night at Trader Vic's in Dallas and worked three summers at the Dallas world headquarters of Dr. Pepper, both on the delivery trucks and in the bottling plant. What jobs did you do on the way to something else? One thing I learned with certainty was that I needed to complete my studies, get a degree, and develop a plan.

Not everyone comes to the same conclusion. We may come to the end of our formal education, but the school of hard knocks is always in session. Some find their way and proceed to the next stages with more wins than losses. Others, not so much. "Is there life after high school?" may mark this crucial stage of life.[64]

Friendships are an important part of this first leg of the adult journey. Friends of all kinds cannot be overestimated. Think about the ensemble TV shows that target this age group. Those without a gaggle of friends suffer in silence and isolation. For many, we only come to know ourselves through our interactions with others whom we trust and love who also share our pathway to adulthood. These friends are our first defense in the nurturing of self, as they are fully understanding of our first failures and serve as the cheering crowds with whom we celebrate our first successes.

Love is a major theme at this stage. Love and sex are paramount! Old mores hold little power as the past has given way to the future. The relationship rules for the young are different from those of the old, and there's no going back. There is a deep wish for intimacy, and this is a major focus of concern for exploring relationships that take priority over other interests, but many feel as though they don't have enough outlets by which to encounter possible love interests. The shot clock on this initiative winds down with cruelty as the apparent window of opportunity closes. Some settle, while others hold out for a miracle to happen.

Another theme is identity—a way of understanding who we are and why we exist. For the first time in their lives, people in this stage of young adulthood may have a three-dimensional way of understanding themselves that includes the meta-narrative of their ongoing stories, tying together the past, present, and future. By accepting where they are at this moment, they may come to understand more appreciably where they've come from and, hopefully, accept where they're headed. (Note that the angst they may feel upon having this three-dimensional self-knowledge may produce dark feelings of loss that mark the latter years of young adulthood and stain the early years of middle adulthood. I will forestall discussing this angst until Essay Seven.)

Between my freshman and sophomore years of college, I was given responsibilities as a leader among the high school youth group on their summer mission trip. I was not the leader, but the youth minister allowed me agency to lead and influence those who were barely younger than me. When I say I was given agency, I mean my youth minister gave me room to lead and respected the decisions I made in the tasks of the week. What happened during the week's activities affirmed a sense of calling that opened a wholly different way of viewing the direction of my life. At the end of a long day with a lively youth group and all their activities, my youth minister and I sat up late after everyone else had gone to bed. We discussed the day and also explored the first feelings that I would label "a calling in life." From that experience and those strategic conversations, I went back to college and began moving in directions that were shaped by my experience as a leader, someone who had a calling in life. By December after this experience, I had withdrawn from one university and enrolled in another to follow that new direction. I changed majors. I changed my limited view of myself, began fleshing out a new course of study, and followed the wind that was blowing fresh in my life. That singular summer experience opened a whole new world for me. That one experience sent my life in new directions, and I had a sense of calling by which I was able to take decided steps along a new path. I encountered new friends on this path who would become my colleagues for a lifetime of work. At the time, I knew we were friends, but I had no way of knowing our friendships would continue over decades of life's experiences. How could I know this at the time?

I met and married a woman I encountered within this new vision of myself and in this new direction I had taken. We are married still and untouched by many of the tragedies some of our friends have faced. Together we encountered our infertility, and so we adopted a son and, two and a half years later, produced a daughter because we lived in a time of fertility miracles. "Making babies" was never so complicated. Having a direction gave me new life and created a completely new future.

Richard Rohr suggests that the task of the first half of life is to create a proper *container* for one's life and to answer the first quintessential questions: What makes me significant? How can I support myself? Who will go with me? The container is not an end in itself, but it exists for the sake of one's deeper and fullest life, which one largely does not know about oneself. The task of the second half of life is to find the *contents* that this container was meant to hold and deliver.[65] Rohr probes the core issues of younger adults who are trying to piece together a direction in life and explores how they intend to relate to the key figures they've enlisted as friends, lovers, and cohorts. If one can make a path toward a meaningful challenge, one will begin to build the platform that will guide one to a complete life. This is the period when the right friends, the right adventurers, can add meaning to a fragile but exciting time.

Time looks open-ended, but it is fractional and brief before it morphs into something unexpected. Life can seem full of possibility in the transition from the last of adolescence, as one begins to live a fully adult life with its responsibilities and opportunities. But it can also sour as one realizes that the life one is expected to live comes with a cost that one must address by joining adulthood at the lowest rung with its limited income and high-end expenses. How does one prepare for these challenges? The responsibilities of adulthood are surprising and severe as one moves away from the security of a home where food was readily available and the utilities were always on to now becoming the supplier of these things without a clear sense of what is needed and how much one needs to succeed. The transition from the home provided by one's parents to funding one's own place is difficult for most first-timers on their own. But beyond that, true independence comes when one is able to handle the occasional surprise house repair or to absorb the predictable breakdown of the car, all of which takes big bites out of one's short savings.

For a variety of reasons, this sort of independence is a huge hurdle for a younger adult to manage. Some fail miserably as their income is either not handled sufficiently for the challenge or is simply not enough to fund the lifestyle the younger adult wants to sustain. For many young adults, the realities of low pay, high housing costs, and high medical bills keep them from attaining this sort of economic independence. These are all huge life challenges, and it surprises no one that some suffer immensely in making mistakes—or suffering setbacks—that are not fatal but can be crippling.

With too many mistakes or setbacks, and you lose a job and even your first home or apartment, swamped with too many bills and too few funds. This can be the first stages of humiliation in which younger adults end up back home with parents or on the couch of a friend, a dislocation that may be allowed for a brief time before they are eventually rejected. Going home can be difficult because relationships must be renegotiated. Absorbing the strain of unpaid debts and the subsequent crash of one's credit ratings can literally hobble the future for months or years as one learns how punitive these losses can become. But what shall these young adults do? How do they lick their wounds and rebuild their lives? All of these experiments in risk and failure become the learning loops for the rest of their lives.

Poet Mary Oliver asks, "What is it you plan to do with your one wild and precious life?" This poet's probing question concerns our self-awareness, the wisdom we might possess, and the level of clarity we bring to our life purposes. We can find meaning in almost any circumstances if we have uncovered a glimpse of who we are and where we are headed. But those glimpses are terribly difficult to acquire at such a young age! These are the challenges of the day, and we must narrow the focus of life onto answering these questions if we are to move with confidence into the future.

What are the rituals that mark young adulthood? The struggles of adolescence have been faced. Some finish their formal education in adolescence, and some are still hard at it well into adulthood. Some leave adolescence and move into a job or even a career. Some find a love interest. Some get married, but many do not. Matters of sexuality and romance are begun in adolescence, but in young adulthood, they become more serious and have greater meaning. Young adults are waiting later and later to make a commitment to a life partner. The old paradigms of sexuality (the rules of the game) have changed radically and will likely never revert to the old expectations. Young adulthood is a time of "finding oneself." Handed-down beliefs are challenged. One will likely keep some of these beliefs—but not all of them. Religious beliefs are sometimes not carried forward into young adulthood, as leaving home may imply that one will choose to leave their faith. Unchallenged, meaningless beliefs are jettisoned for no faith or indifferent faith. This is true on almost every frontier of life.

At the end of this first adult stage is the move toward middle adulthood. It is not terrain we recognize until it's too late. We find ourselves at the middle of what life may give us. We face an existential moment of concern, and certain age markers can overshadow the relative joy of younger adulthood. Before we know it, before we can do anything about it, we are facing the signposts that declare we are leaving one stage and entering another.

What happens at the middle of anything? What are the implications, good or bad? What other "midpoint experiences" can you recall, and how are they made meaningful through some ritual? Perhaps it's the halfway point of a long car drive. You may see yourself as halfway between first and second base. It's that moment at the end of your sophomore year, and you may celebrate being "halfway home" in completing your degree. Generally, we don't pay attention to too many midpoints, except when it comes to age. In becoming "middle aged," we miss recognizing it by clinging to our sense of youth in some overly generous, overcompensating way.

The signs of our aging as young adults may be subtle despite the pounds we put on or the nagging issues of hair (too little in some places and too much in other unexpected places) or the decline in our overall physical condition. We're also showing signs that we will eventually look like our parents even if we don't see it ourselves. Likely soon, they themselves will begin looking like grandparents.

When the circle of life closes one stage, another comes to take its place. It is a death and a birth all over again. As we come to terms with the signs of aging and other forms of loss, may we realize that the seeds for the future have already been planted and new growth will come to bear fruit.

Story Starters: Young Adulthood

• **Leftovers from Adolescence.** How did your family ritualize your move from (partial) dependence to (partial) independence and/or interdependence during the previous stage of adolescence? What ritual, if any, did your family observe to help you realize you now had the keys to your own life? How old were you when this happened? Did your parents also recognize this stage, or did you come to this knowledge at different times? How did the family rituals of your childhood and adolescence need to adapt and change? Did any new rituals emerge to replace them?

• **Social Life and Friends.** In what ways did your friends replace your family? How did your family rituals become friend rituals?

• **Lovers.** Love stories abound: sexual experiences, near-miss love commitments, failures and disappointments in love, ensemble friendships. What significant stories do you recall that typify your love life at this stage?

• **Failure and Loss.** When did you first experience personal defeat or significant loss? Loss of a job? Failure at school or admittance to school? What do you recall of how that was ritualized?

• **Choosing a Life Partner.** For many, this is the stage of life where love and romance become entangled with the search for someone with whom you want to share life. Dating, engagement, and marriage—what rituals did you use to recognize each stage? How did you handle shared love or rejected love?

• **Career.** This age is marked by the search for meaningful work. Vocation and calling are often concepts that help shape this consideration. How did you navigate these important decisions?

• **Forgiveness and Reconciliation.** How have you handled the mistakes of young adulthood? Likely, these mistakes were more serious or consequential than those made in adolescence. How did you respond? How did you resolve the complications of your mistakes, and how did you seek reconciliation with others?

• **God.** The idea of God and religious matters comes under the microscope in young adulthood. Many move away from such beliefs, while others find new meaning, often tempered by adult thinking. How did you understand God as a youth? When did your faith in God shift in ways that mirrored your life as an adult? If these changes were experienced as a faith crisis, how did you resolve these things? The faith of childhood must become the faith of adulthood, or perhaps the whole notion of faith is dropped altogether. How has this worked for you?

• **Preparing for Essay Seven.** If you're part of a group, recall your stories of middle adulthood and select a category from the questions suggested at the end of the next session. Come ready with a story to explore!

Journal

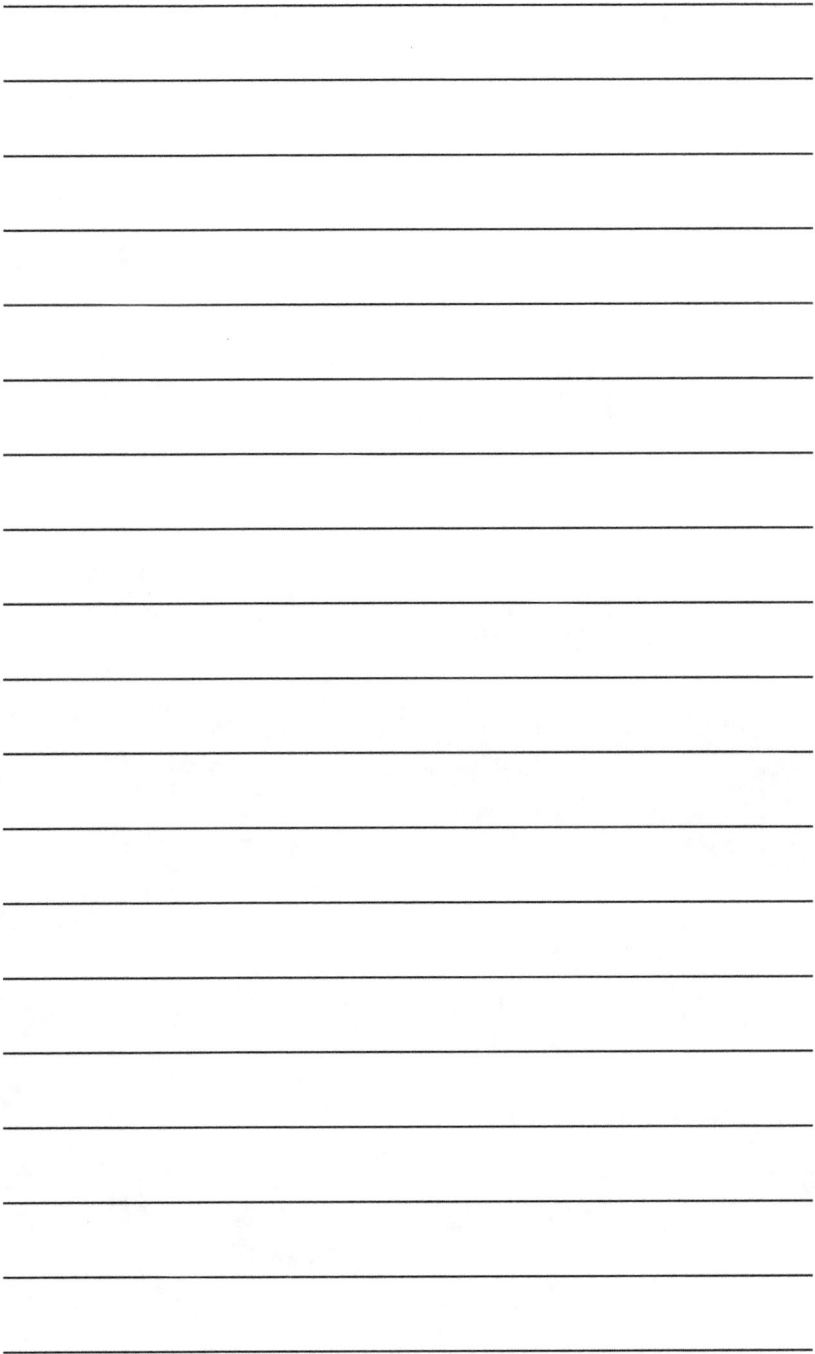

Middle Adulthood– The Fifth and Sixth Decades

I am the one I hardly recognize in the mirror. I first knew I was middle-aged when I bent over to pick something off the floor and heard a sound emanating from deep within. It was not a word but more like a sound I had been muttering for some time and ignored, something I could hold back no longer. "Oomph." A sound I exhaled as if my whole body was sighing from the effort given to simply bending over. I understood that this one sound alone was my signal to no one in particular that just bending over was a big deal. Has it come to that? Yes, it has.

I am halfway around the track and hardly recognize the journey I'm making. I'm not in touch with my own mind, my own body, much less my own spirit. I've mostly given up on finding the right paths. Now I'm hoping simply to make it from sunup to sundown, to make good and decent decisions for myself and for those I love, to do my fair share, to avoid screwing up. I've leveled the challenge of the mountaintops to more humble hilltops, thinking I might occasionally climb to the top of a nearby hill even if I'm no longer scaling tall peaks.

I am the sum total of my gains and my disappointments at this stage. My successes have been fewer than I hoped, and the gains have been modest but sure. I have tried and failed, but Lord knows I have tried. I'm open to suggestions. I'm open to sound advice. I'm open to the good gifts of a true friend and to someone to love who will love me in return The far shore of life is closer now. The realm of possibilities has narrowed, so the choices are clearer.

I have given myself to many essential things. I have a family to feed and care for, to nurture and shape and mold. I have issues that come with reaching the midpoint in life: issues of worth, issues of values, issues of the faint sounds of a ticking clock in the background of everything I do, whether I'm paying attention or not. My issues of self are weighted in judgment about myself, with self-condemnation so pernicious that I project it on everyone around me. I do this unconsciously as a self-soothing attempt, even if those I project upon (particularly those I project upon) are my closest family and friends. The closer I feel to them, the freer I feel about dumping my inner stuff upon them.

Less active and more sedentary, I do a lot of sitting. My best cozy furniture takes on the shape of my backside from the hours I spend sitting there. I sit all evening watching my shows. Even when there's nothing I'm interested in, I watch. The shows I watch are generational because the advertisers have clearly identified me. The commercials are all about healthcare aids and diets and exercise products, about my joints, my mouth, my hearing, and my bowels. These advertisers know me better than I know myself.

I may also read, but admittedly if I read I don't read the heavy stuff, mostly self-help books that range from diets to a romantic life I read about but don't experience. I read histories, mysteries, or an occasional action novel. I have my favorite authors, so I try to keep up. I may or may not read a newspaper; mostly I get my news from late-night comedians.

One surety: I have given myself to work. Hi ho, hi ho, it's off to work I go! I go to bed tired and wake up feeling the weight of the world as I do the same thing today that I did yesterday. I have made my peace with having a boss who watches me and critically assesses my work. I can't quite see retirement, but that doesn't stop me from thinking about it. This is the long middle stretch that seems endless. I can no longer see the starting line, but neither can I see the approaching finish line. I had dreams, but now I only have boredom.

I am caught in the swirl of time, moments that can take forever and seasons that fly by in a rush. How can it be both? I frantically search for meaning but work as if I have secured it. Making meaning is my search for the Holy Grail as I try to interpret my life. I don't do this for anyone but myself.

It's feast or famine. My cup of earnings is either half full or half empty. I may have more assets than I could have imagined at the beginning, but I live in fear that I've not saved nearly enough. I should have started earlier in putting aside a slice of the pie for the future. Is there a point of no return where the concept of "saving enough" becomes an obvious impossibility? I live a fictional dream and enter the Publisher's Clearing House or buy lottery tickets in hopes of winning the jackpot. Is 1:2.4 billion a number or an impossible fantasy? I am more likely to die in an asteroid strike. I may be doing everything right and still feel I'm falling behind and slipping over the edge.

I pray my health will hold up, but I'm already experiencing the slight pangs of blood pressure, cholesterol, heart concerns, diabetes, or even a round of cancer. My bathroom cabinet is crowded with medications and vitamins and supplements. There's a payment due for this stage of life, and I'm hoping to have what it takes to keep it all in perspective. I join a health club and swear I'll do better this year. I'm good for a few weeks, and then I backslide. The weight of gravity bears down ever so slowly on my joints, my posture, even my face. Everything seems to be sliding downward.

No doubt there are challenges in these middle years, and those challenges are substantial. While I may face my share of declines and losses, there will be times to celebrate. As my children grow to adolescence and young adulthood, I will watch how they emerge with a healthy sense of themselves. I see them adopt their own values by which they will take hold of their own journey. Perhaps my efforts at work are blossoming and I can be confident in my accomplishments. If I'm particularly fortunate, I may even continue to grow in my love for the person with whom I have made deep commitments. In this age of the whole range of experiences, I hope and pray to find balance. I pray for the wisdom to recognize the true nature of my life and to accept my life for what it is ... an amazing gift.

❦

No doubt about it, the middle passage sneaks up on us. If you're wondering whether you're there, you likely are. When did you first realize you were middle aged? How hard was it to accept this as true? John Claypool describes this as "the most strenuous segment of our existence. If adolescence is the most intense stage along the way, I would say that adulthood is the most demanding. Not only is it so long, it also involves so many different challenges *simultaneously* [emphasis mine]."[66] My son declared on my forty-ninth birthday, "Gee, Dad, in a decade you'll be sixty!" Nothing like the hubris of a twenty-something son with his old man.

These are the middle years of the longest segment of the human journey known collectively as adulthood. The mid-forties to the mid-sixties is the stage Gail Sheehy calls simply "the middle life." This is the second act, a second adulthood. This is the age when the seeds of the past are in a delicate dance with the seeds of the future. We have worked diligently in making something of ourselves, first in school and then in work. We have built something out of the bits and pieces of life as we see it, but maybe something is missing.

We come to see that we have become this or that, but still our interior "me" is barely formed. Perhaps we've lived someone else's life more than our own. We've followed the paths that were presented to us by our parents, our teachers, our love partners. Maybe the risk of finding out what we really want to do in life has been withheld from our forward thoughts and we have instead lived a different life. This middle passage may be a time of renewal when we finally come to ask ourselves what we want to do or be. The idea that "nothing is wasted" is a hopeful lifeline as we recalibrate the direction of our lives. Some come to this wisdom easier than others, and some wait too late to make these changes. How do you move forward into a new direction when you have people—your life partner and your children, a business partner or others—who depend on you to stay the course? The window of opportunity may close quickly, and we may need to make peace with the paths we have taken. Our identity may or may not be reflected in what we do in life to support us and those to whom we are committed, but it's a beginning step in that direction.

What markers help us imagine this stage of middle adulthood? There is the push of the past and the pull of the future. For those who have found the path on which they wish to walk, this can be a fruitful time. For others, however, it can be shaky, and they may spin their wheels but see no noticeable progress. It's a time to make progress because the needs of the future demand it. For many, there are fault lines at work, in friendships, and particularly in their families. People in their middle years can make peace with where life is being lived, but many view these years as a struggle. Welcome to the ambiguity of the middle stage of adulthood!

Undoubtedly, the second half of life is different from the first half. Carl Jung mapped this age by contrasting the first half of life as climbing the mountain with the second half as descending. One question Claypool asks is, "Where are the navigational charts for the descent . . . that will sustain a person in the afternoon and evening of life?"[67] In young adulthood, we are establishing an identity and a home, building relationships with people who exist in our lives as friends and whom we serve as a community, searching for security, and building a platform for our lives.

In leaving adolescence, how many of us have a clear idea of which direction we will take in life? Who can imagine anything beyond the near horizon and learning to trust they will find the way through the next stages? It appears we make decisions that create the future, not that we choose a sharply defined future and then carve the path toward that desired end. Looking back, it seems that I made hundreds of pivotal decisions that created my future; by being engaged, seeking to make good decisions in the farmer's corn maze, and trusting in the goodness of life, I would eventually find my way.

Psychotherapist Robert Johnson identifies the unseen decisions, the intrusive events, and the happenstance of life as "the slender threads."[68] The way he describes it, the slender threads are the seemingly unanticipated events or occurrences evident in what we view as the everyday. One doesn't need to be a person of faith to recognize that the slender threads may be the signs of a larger hand guiding us all into an unplanned future. Call it faith. Call it destiny. Call it providence. Making meaning is the challenge in those moments. How else do we explain the unexplainable? Key people in my life have unknowingly shined a light on the path to my eventual future. Opportunities have come my way that opened one door after another toward new directions that I might never have selected for myself. Events have unfolded that swept me up in a wave and carried me to unplanned shores. To be sure, I have been a partner to these slender threads by acting in sync with each opportunity, using my wisdom in making decisions both good and bad, but I have not been in control of all things—just present and alert to the direction the winds may take me.

In the pivotal arenas, I have enjoyed the rich blessing of knowing others who may or may not have understood the effect they were having on me. Typically, these people were significant only at one particular time, but their cumulative effect tilted the direction of my life by giving me opportunities for growth and experience.

The midpoint of life is a gracious opportunity for one to assess what their gifts in life are or to at least reassess whether they wish to work on new habits. The gift of hope for the future comes from somewhere outside of ourselves. Where does your hope come from? Others have an insatiable thirst for knowledge and have kept learning over the years. Who taught you to keep learning? Some are encouragers who keep their eyes open to congratulate or point out when others have succeeded. Who shaped this life-giving sense of encouragement in them?

Curiosity may take place in the form of connecting the dots, as if life is a puzzle to be solved. I became open to new insights about old events as I looked in the rearview mirror and saw the directional signs I had followed in making meaning. I have not been successful in every arena, but I can see how the sum total of my adventures has taken cues from both failures and successes to make sense of what has happened. I've learned to incorporate it all—the successes and the failures—as part and parcel of how my life has been lived.

This is not singularly true of any one stage, but it has likely been the way of my whole life from beginning to end. Interspersed with uncountable ordinary experiences, there are key moments, strategic occurrences, and the involvement of people who have acted in benevolent ways toward those around them. Key figures for me have been educators who were available to me for more than just the curriculum. Grandparents, ministers, scout leaders, and other community leaders have inexplicably adopted me for collegial relationships to offer affirmation and friendship. We cannot overestimate the ways in which our lives have grown in new directions from such simple, powerful relationships. All of these summary ideas reflect how our lives are interwoven with those around us. We are a part of the web of friends and even our opponents who are bound together by covenants, by happenstance, and by the slender threads that seek to bring us into relationships with significant others, all of whom play a role in our being, our joy, and our losses. None of us exist in isolation; all of us live an interconnected life.

Something happens that turns our attention away from first-half accomplishments toward something deeper, something that alters our life's trajectory. At a key point, the supposed achievements of individuation or identity fall apart and show themselves to be lacking. We come to a blockade, and our progress slows or halts. Richard Rohr, like many others with the interpretive skills for this stage of life, has noted, "Normally a job, fortune or reputation has to be lost, a death has to be suffered, a house has to be flooded, or a disease has to be endured."[69] Rohr calls this as a form of "falling," or what he calls "necessary suffering."

I served for six years as pastor of a church of which my older colleagues remarked, "Whoever goes there will be the church's last pastor." While that assessment seems harsh, it was a clinical analysis of the congregational context and the widely known belief that the church had chosen a future path that would deliver them to the point of failure. No doubt the church had made some questionable choices in the decade prior to this moment in time, but they still had assets one might consider enough to stave off dissolution. One of my colleagues even suggested, "On the first day you go there, redo your resume and go back to looking for your next church. You'll need to be looking to move to save your family."

The church had given considerable thought to relocating from their historical neighborhood, which had changed from a predominantly upper-middle class population to an area of rundown homes and a changing demographic. Community pride and historical appreciation can only go so far when the possibilities of the past are no longer present. I worked steadily for four years trying to guide us to being invested in the immediate neighborhood, but we were so foreign to the new community that we had few options to grow as a means of covering our losses. On the day we held the funeral for what I call a load-bearing church member, I remember walking down the staff hallway and, as I passed our financial secretary, hearing her mutter under her breath, "That one hurt." No explanation was needed, as she was acknowledging that the death of this member meant fewer financial gifts, an immediate hit on our budget. Downsizing was a style of ministry we were facing, and each year we lost significant members who had given their lives to making the church wonderful.

It finally dawned on a small handful of leaders that we could make a deliberate response to the harsh reality that the church would eventually fail, or we could continue to bleed to death. We began our discussions and determined a path or two that we might follow. Eventually, this led to our hard-fought decision to sell our buildings to an inner-city church that needed the kind of location we currently held. Over a six-month period, we held strategic conversations with this church and made the difficult decision to sell to them at a price that would enable them to have the highest chance of being successful. The sacrificial act of selling meant that the mission of the church would be honored even if one church had to let go of itself in order for the move to occur.

One Sunday, I found myself preaching the last sermon in our church and facing an immediate search for a new place of ministry. The rise and fall of these circumstances was a laboratory in the nature of ministry, affording me a new appreciation of how success and failure might be measured and giving me a place where I could learn as a minister how to embody the depths of such issues. Nearly a year later, I was called to a new church in the Midwest, in a place I didn't know I was looking for, and my life and my family's lives were altered in altogether new directions. Seldom did I believe I had failed, although that question haunted me until I finally recognized that, in truth, I had succeeded. I was not the person I was before, and my life's trajectory was cast in a new light and toward an unrecognized future. Only in hindsight does this experience begin to make sense.

Most of us live our lives backing into the future, making the choices of each new moment based on the data and agenda of the old. This explains why repetitive patterns turn up in our lives. Søren Kierkegaard noted in his journal the paradox that life must be remembered backward but lived forward. Carl Jung humorously noted that we all live in shoes too small for us. We exist within the boundaries of old strategies and unwittingly become the enemies of our own growth, our own largess of soul, through our repetitive history-bound choices. It is far easier to walk in shoes too small for us than to step into the largeness the soul expects and demands. By the middle passage, we are ready to reflect on how our lives are made and how our choices create our futures, and to reconsider a new path to take. The middle passage is understood when we discern that our repetitions, compensations, and treatment plans have their origin not in conscious life but in unconscious history.

Psychotherapist James Hollis claims that living through the middle passage requires two practices: we must take responsibility for ourselves (stop blaming others), and we must look within to see the repetitive core ideas, complexes, and historic influences that point out where the true enemy lies.[70] All of us are fighting demons of one kind or another, enemies of our true self, causing us to live below what our gifts in life would suggest is a stronger self. Specifically, Hollis wrote, "The flight from ourselves will always mean that we will be uncomfortable with another. What we fear in ourselves we will fear in the other; what we avoid addressing in ourselves we will avoid in the other; where we are stuck with ourselves we will be stuck with the other."[71]

This perspective seems to point toward the issue of projection, as I take my own concerns and fears and anxieties and project them upon those around me in ways I cannot recognize. This projection is an invitation to know myself at my deepest levels so I can understand that I am doing this unconsciously. To raise the unconscious to the conscious is more than a catchphrase. Projection is useful to consider in any relationship with others, as they are often doing the same thing, and their strange and awkward behavior may be an indication that they are projecting their own broken selves upon me or upon others. Here's how John Claypool described this confluence:

> There is an awesome interconnectedness to the various stages of life. What we are to be in the future we are now becoming, which means that agedness is not as remote and unrelated as we might think just because

we are twenty or thirty or forty . . . we do not wait until we are sixty-five to begin to get ready.[72]

The seeds of the future are always planted in the now, awaiting a day when they will germinate and intertwine our stages of life.

Illuminative stories from literature help us flesh out this stage. Larry McMurtry, in his many novels, has written a series of stories that describe the arc of life, or at least the arc from adolescence to older adulthood.[73] His highly regarded *The Last Picture Show* is likely the most widely known work of this collection, either from the book itself or from the award-winning movie. He creates strong characters as one story evolves into the next, one promised sequel after another, through five novels that trace a handful of characters from adolescence across the arc of life. In what some have called "the Thalia stories," a series of novels centered in a fictional North Texas oil town (perhaps related to McMurtry's hometown of Archer City), he gives us a cast of characters that revolve around oilman Duane Moore. From his adolescence forward, Duane lives a desperate existence across the first half of his adulthood, but he continues to grow in the series, especially as he confronts his inner sense of self as lived in contrast to the arid oil patch where there are as many pickup trucks as there are people. This is a bleak landscape where the blue-collar folks are predictably bored by the limited life dramas observed from the windows of the local Dairy Queen or the occasional stopovers at the country convenience store. These characters are rich in personality and illustrate how people can explore their own sense of meaning.

In *Duane's Depressed*, Duane turns sixty-two and realizes he has spent enough of his life riding in his pickup back and forth from oil rig to oil rig in the oil patch and has grown bored and tired of his worthless adult kids and their equally worthless children. All of these colorful offspring have latched onto Duane and his wife Karla for funding their vapid, dependent lives. As he crosses the last of middle age, his wife Karla diagnoses Duane with depression. In a moment of clarity about his life, he tosses his truck keys into a ceramic coffee cup and strikes out walking. Later he takes up riding an expensive high-tech bicycle on which he traverses the country-side. He ends up moving out of the house where he feels trapped by his life, trapped by his wife and their children and grandchildren, and into a one-room hunting shack with his dog. Most of his family and friends are convinced he has lost his sanity, but Duane has come to a late-blooming sense of what he should do with himself, and his actions are focused on the changes that help him reorient himself to what his life should come to be. Duane has come to the end of one life, and he takes up a new direction. He simplifies the trappings of the life he has made in the years leading up to this point, and now he determines that he will not live out his days in the old ruts that were grooved in his unreflective life.

McMurtry paints the crisis of self this way:

> What happened to him [Duane] had nothing to do with a deterioration in his major relationships. Even to say something simplistic, such as that it was time for a change, would not be stating the matter accurately. It wasn't that it was *time* for a change, particularly; it was that he had just *changed*. . . . He didn't become a different man, but when he stepped out of his house he found himself in a different life . . . . He had just walked off: with no animosity toward anyone, with no intent to harm, wishing everybody well—just walked off. He knew it must be puzzling to everybody, but he couldn't help that. The change had just come, as naturally as a change in the weather—one day cloudy, one day fair.[74]

It's obvious the storyteller has the power to shine a light on the challenges of this strained stage in which one comes face to face with the fault lines of a life and change must be addressed. In the fictional life of Duane Moore, we have a model for reflection. The actions he takes are abrupt but purposeful. He moves away from a cumulative brokenness in his interior world and chooses to ignore the bad advice of others who love him but who can't be silent about their disapproval. Could this be a model for us to understand that we must change in order to survive? In the interconnected world of a family, we can see how the web of others can powerfully resist our impulses to change. At the fruitful stage where personal reflection can lead us to rethink our lives, our family and friends can resist the changes that are essential to the new directions we want to explore and that call for our commitment to chart our own new paths.

The changes Duane sought had less to do with his wife, Karla, and their extended brood of kids and grandkids. His oil patch company continued on and became less dependent on him. In other words, his decision to alter the direction of his life was inside of him. Over time, he had shriveled and grown stale. His changes led him to open his eyes and take charge of his inner world. These changes were relatively minor but were cosmic in how he viewed himself and the role he played in it. Duane turned his back on the zombie life he was living and chose to grow.

In the second half of life, we must embrace two major tasks:[75] the recovery of personal authority and the discovery of personal spirituality. We have finally lived enough of life that we can bring these tasks into sharper focus. Those who embrace these needs will find both energy to explore them and also resistance to make the changes needed or desired. The energy unleashed by change will be a matter of will. We do not need to be prompted about these needs (we're not children), but each person will find their own path and will feel compelled to tackle these issues with diligence. A convergence occurs in this middle passage that is signified by life experience, a strong presence of both successes and failures, and a desire to make meaning out of where we now stand in relation to the middle ground between the first and second halves of our lives. Perhaps we realize we have been living someone else's life, that their demands are being lived out, directing our values and decisions. A brief description of this middle-age challenge is to deconstruct our false self. Jung describes this challenge as something that happens when we realize we have made the long climb to the middle stage and are now ready to descend the path we have taken. We have finally come to the crisis of change as the goals and tasks in the stage of life we inhabit have shifted. The goal of childhood is to become an individual, and the goal of adulthood is to give that individuality away. The task of childhood is to separate while the task of adulthood is to connect.[76]

Many experience this crisis of change in the middle years after they reawaken an awareness of their lives through deep reflection about how they have lived the journey thus far. All the struggle to create a life lived without reflection must give way to the courage to go in new directions in order to recover themselves and fulfill their calling in life. This may be experienced as an itch, a twitch, a subtle demand, or a deep inner yearning. No matter—we must give ourselves to making the needed changes, or we will die. How one accepts the challenge of change will vary from person to person. Some will choose symbolic actions that point to an inner shift they are following, such as acquiring a tattoo of deep meaning, accepting a challenge they've put off such as hiking the Appalachian Trail or taking a pilgrimage such as the Camino de Santiago in Spain. Some will leave the work that has consumed them for the last several decades and do something altogether different—go to law school or start a soup kitchen or open a bike shop. Some will savor the work of new poets or take up karate. Some will make new friends or refuse to live within the expectations of people they don't respect. Some will complete an unfinished degree or restore a broken relationship. Some will grow their hair long or cut it all off, grow a beard, wear bow ties, or write a book. The point is not so much the thing itself but what it means. Listen again to the wisdom of the poet who asks, "Tell me, what is it you plan to do / with your one wild and precious life?"[77] or face the challenge of the writer who observed, "The place God calls you to is the place where your deep gladness and the world's deep hunger meet."[78]

The first task of middle adulthood is to recover our personal authority. In the beginning, we were naïve and dependent to the point that narcissism was considered normal. In childhood and adolescence, we resisted the need to own our lives, to make our own choices, and to take responsibility for those choices. We incorporated the values and demands of others, but may have given away too much of ourselves. Individuals must make their own assessment about this issue to see whether a course correction is needed to find their original selves and make room for their own needs, to be true to themselves and less conforming to how others want to alter them for their own needs. To recover our personal authority, we accept responsibility for what we make of life. James Hollis claims that we "move from victimhood to participation in the meaning of our journey, and to recognize that in all events, even the traumatic, there is an invitation to greater engagement with depth, with mystery."[79] What constitutes personal authority? Most simply, it is to find what is true for oneself and to live in the world according to those values and those choices.

Honest, experiential spirituality will stretch us and sometimes test us, but it will always ask us to be larger than we may wish to be. Staid religious language, core ideas that have lost their meaning, and our personal beliefs unrevised since childhood are fixed when we cling to our outgrown concrete thinking. The problem many believers face is that they've outgrown their faith and have not nurtured an adult way of believing. Discovering personal spirituality may mean that one is willing to face faith anew with adult sensibilities that include the capacity to ask big questions. Even Paul, the church's first serious correspondent, came to see this need: "When I was a child, I spoke like a child, I thought like a child, I reasoned like a child; when I became an adult, I put an end to childish ways" (1 Cor 13:11, NRSV). Many religious systems are experienced as fixed thinking, and some people may resist the urge—the need—to face our childhood beliefs as a sign of unfaith. If we do not do the hard work of finding a personal spirituality that fits the challenges of their lives, however, we will live a faith that is trapped in concrete thinking, literalizing mythic stories as if they were meant to be fact-based rather than deep mysteries for exploring and testing.

Mature spirituality seldom provides us with certitude, but it will seek the honesty to ask ever-larger questions. Do larger questions lead us to a larger life, or is the challenge of a larger life such that we are forced to confront larger questions? Both are necessary if we are to flourish in the middle passage. In recent years, psychologists have been exploring this midpoint in adulthood and raising critical questions we can use to explore the common issues. In particular, Hollis helps us focus on meaning by recognizing that religious questions are formed by existential concerns. Consider these questions he raises:

> What has brought you to this place in your journey, this moment in your life? What gods, what forces, what family, what social environment, has framed your reality, perhaps supported, perhaps constricted it? Whose life have you been living? . . . Why does the idea of your soul trouble you, and feel familiar as a long-lost companion? Why is the life you are living too small for the soul's desire? Why is now the time, if ever it is to happen, for you to answer the summons of the soul, the invitation to the second, larger life?[80]

Story Starters: Middle Adulthood

• **Leftovers from Young Adulthood.** If the first half of life is defined by climbing the mountain, how does the view look from this point in the middle passage? How would reaching the summit be experienced in ritual form? Was your acceptance of the middle passage celebrated or mourned? How did you mark this moment with friends or family?

• **Social Life.** Our social lives are mostly built around work and family. Which is the dominant domain, and which is secondary? What kinds of events do you use to celebrate accomplishments or significant moments? How do you mark the struggles or defeats together? Are there recurring events that you plan on a regular basis in order to gather together?

• **Holidays and Birthdays.** Paul wrote, "When I became an adult, I put away childish things" (1 Cor 13:11). How do you regard your experience of holidays and birthdays as an adult? How are they the same as such moments in childhood? How do they differ?

• **Friends.** What rituals have you practiced or observed around the ongoing cycle of relationships (gained or lost), such as those with friends, neighbors, or coworkers?

• **Failure and Loss.** When did you first experience personal defeat or significant loss such as the loss of a job? Did you experience failure at school or fail at admittance to school? What do you recall of how that was ritualized?

• **Life Partners/Marriage.** For many, this is the stage of life when love/romance becomes complicated or conflicted with the demands of living with someone to whom we've committed ourselves. Have any rituals emerged that define your relationship with one another? How did you express the end of a relationship? In what ways do you celebrate your love for one another in order to renew your relationship?

• **Career and Vocation.** This age is marked by the search for meaningful work. Vocation and calling are often concepts that help shape this consideration. (You choose a career, but a vocation chooses you.) When that happens, it produces rightness of the soul and harmony within. Vocation is a summons to the divine in you. Joseph Campbell calls this "finding your bliss." How does the idea of finding your vocation/bliss apply to you? How do you express your sense of bliss?

• **Change or Not?** There's an old saying that "you become more and more what you already are." Can you see how the seeds of who you are now were planted early in life? Do you believe this is true? How does one make changes in life, habits, thoughts/beliefs, attitudes? What intentional changes have you made in your life based on some new insight you have about yourself?

• **Identity.** Men in particular are conditioned to think of themselves as synonymous with their work (that's why layoffs, downsizing, and retirement almost always produce depression for men). Women are usually emotionally differentiated (with much keener awareness of their emotions, friends who are supportive of their growth, and a greater ability to explore their own feelings). How do you see this as true or not true of your own relationship to your work?

• **Forgiveness and Reconciliation.** How did you handle the mistakes of young adulthood? Likely, these mistakes were more serious or consequential than those made in adolescence. How did you resolve the complications of your mistakes?

• **God.** How did you understand God as a person in middle age? How has your faith in God shifted in ways that mirror your life as an adult? If these changes were experienced as a faith crisis, how did you resolve it? How did the family or faith community help you understand God? What rituals did you observe that helped you experience God? How did you feel about that practice?

• **Preparing for Essay Eight.** If you are part of a group, recall your stories of older adulthood and select a category from the questions suggested at the end of the next session. Come ready with a story to explore!

Journal

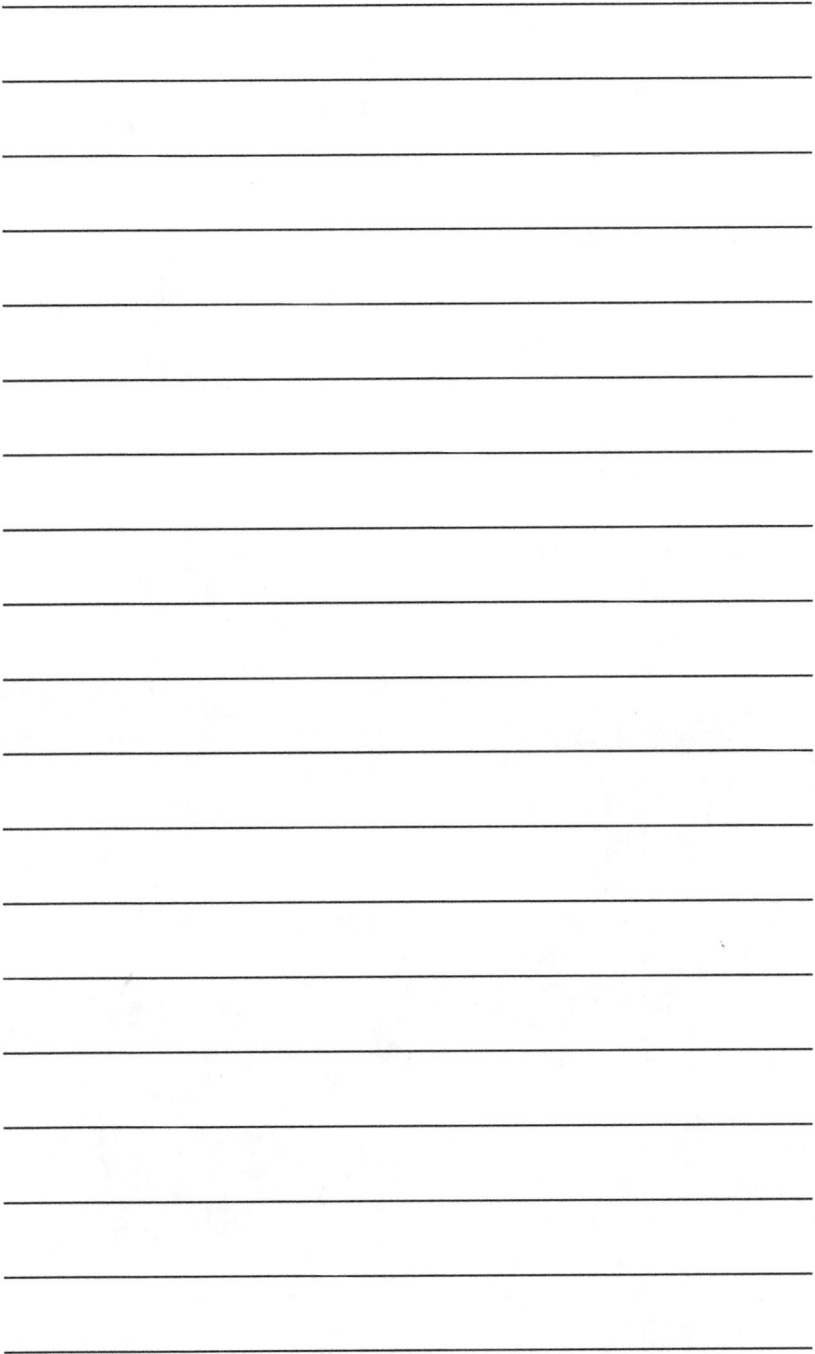

Older Adulthood–The Seventh Decade and Beyond

I am the sum total of my decisions, like seeds cast broadside in the world. All across the arc of life, I cast mindless seeds that continue to bear fruit while others more weighted with expectations fall on the ground to no effect. I am the one who enters this last stage (this "terminal" stage, mind you) with remorse and regrets about more than a few things, and yet in my best moments I feel enormous gratitude. The way I tilt toward one or the other is an indication of my attitude toward life.

I am the one who now understands the contract of life with all its codices and provisions. I was presumptive in not reading the fine print because I was forever busy ignoring such trivialities. The contract of life is now fully known as I look over my shoulder and see the paths my life has taken—all the turns, all the forks in the road, all the cul-de-sac paths that led nowhere. I've been walking this trail all my life, and in looking back, I can see it all. I can see where I made foolish decisions, and I can see the fortuitous paths taken, choices that help me recognize the slender threads of the unseen hand at work on my behalf. All my life has been leading to this point. Everything is connected to everything else. There's an amazing interconnectedness to all things at this stage. In younger stages of wonderment, I couldn't imagine what it would be like in this last stage, but now there's no more wondering. I'm all that and more. What has been fuzzy has now become clear.

The metrics of time are confounding. If I don't have something to keep me busy, I'll go crazy. My days on this earth are numbered, so I try to live with purpose even if I look like I'm doing absolutely nothing. I'm the one who's coming to the end of my time at work, my time consumed by appearances, what others think about me, patience, or even politeness. Hitting sixty was confusing. Does this mean I have to give up my middle adult privileges? Claiming a senior discount doesn't quite pay for the reality of it all.

If I've technically crossed over from the middle passage, why do I feel so good? I'm all for keeping an eye on the near horizon, but I can't remember being this confused about where I stand. I'm too old to ignore all this, but I'm also living in a younger person's body and can still do everything I ever did and feel just like I've felt for the last twenty-five years. Which am I?

I am the one who can be gentle and kind or abruptly short and snippy. I can be opinionated and can show no signs of remorse when I hurt someone's feelings. I can be sugary sweet with children and merciless when they act in ways that irritate me. I live in a principled world. Why aren't the children in my life being taught how to behave in public?

I have more doctors than friends, more medications than wrinkles or age spots, of which I have plenty. I may have hobbies and interests that keep me younger than my friends, or I may shrink into a smaller and smaller world until there's only the room I live in. I have family but worry about the useless way they live, about the behavior of their wild kids, and about why they don't come visit.

I hold great wisdom from a lifetime of paying attention to how things really are in the world. I have immersed myself into life and have been a traveler through this world. I have wisdom about how the world works and about who I am as one who has earned the right to know who I am.

This last stage could end tomorrow, or it could end up being the longest adult stage of all, depending on my genes and on the way fate or luck or karma plays itself out in my life. For a while I worried whether I would first run out of days or out of money, but now I don't see the point in fretting about it and just get up every morning to a new day. I figure I can either get absorbed by fatalism or embrace the wonder of another day. Adventures abound, and I can greet each morning wide-eyed with wonder or I can fall into the abyss. What would you do?

At the end of this age is the beyond, of which I have little idea what to expect. Everyone's got an opinion, but no one has the insider's knowledge to know much of anything for certain. The philosophers are skeptics, but their imaginations are just as vivid as those of true believers of religion. My old professor would mutter, "You pays your money and you takes your choice." The best religion seems to offer on the great mysteries are promises wrapped up in metaphors and stories and analogies. That's it. No comfort in science, no verifiable uncontested statements of fact . . . only poetry and hymns and the testimony of a handful of the saints to assure us. "Things hoped for," the Good Book tells us, and "the conviction of things not seen." For people of faith, it's enough. We hold on to our candles of truth and love, and we cling to the mercy of God. Even if I've lived across the arc in denial, at this stage in life, some of the church's best lines have fallen flat. Here I am living in the fading light of life, hoping it's enough. I may not be ready when my moment comes, but I am here.[81] When the moment comes, I want to have enough awareness to see it coming and enough courage to welcome it. I want the day of my death to mirror the day of my birth. The great mystery is the long passage, the doorway that leads me . . . where? How will the final passage be for me? Will it be like being born? Will it be fearful or all goodness and light? I am standing on the platform awaiting the train to pull into the station, and when it arrives for me, the doors will open and I will be ushered in for this great journey. I am ready.

⁘

The border between middle and older adulthood is not finely drawn; even so, there are the obvious markers of work and family and energy and well-being to help one know that a crossing is being made. Paul Tournier observed that one of those markers is an awareness of time. People in this last stage come to see that time itself is diminishing, and once spent that time cannot be recovered.[82] The window of opportunity slowly but surely begins to close on dreams and on the wish for accomplishments that might secure our place in the memory of those we want to remember us. Tournier is a pragmatist about all this, as he sees that the die is cast. "That which I have been able to do, to learn, or to acquire is gradually losing its value. The *doing* and the *having* are giving way to the *being*."[83] This is an age of seeking and accepting wisdom. It is an age of coming to terms with all that has been and making peace with how life has been spent.

When do we "cross the divide"? This is an issue we face from stage to stage, but it is never more pertinent than when we cross the divide between our middle and older years. Where is the line? Will we know with certainty when we reach it? How will we recognize this shift, or is it like the other stages, in which one only knows after crossing the divide and seeing it in the rearview mirror? Perhaps it comes when one attains what poet Billy

Collins calls "the big number"? Decadal birthdays have a habit of reorganizing life for us.

What markers help us imagine this stage of older adulthood? Here's a sampler: confronting the ample signs that time is winding down, embracing the significant shift that one must take in order to accept one's authenticity, finding creative ways to embrace the shift away from identity as defined by work and to embrace identity as an extension of one's core, accepting one's declining physical condition while opening up to the new growth that must be chosen, finding new meaning on all boundaries of friendship, family, and faith. People in this last stage of life are given new light to follow, but they struggle with the shadows that accompany this time. Welcome to the ambiguities of the last stage of adulthood!

At the age of seventy, Erik Erikson delivered the Jefferson Lectures in Washington, D.C., in 1973. Those notes were expanded and became his book, *Dimensions of a New Identity*. In the concluding paragraph, he observes about youth, "you find out what you *care to do* and who you *care to be*." In young adulthood, he writes, "you learn whom you *care to be with*," and in (middle) adulthood, "you learn to know what and whom you can *take care of*."[84] Crossing the divide from our middle passage to our older years is recognizing that we are entering a time in life when we struggle between our renewed engagement and apathy. One world is in decline, but another world waits to take its place.

Erikson describes this as the struggle between integrity and despair. In his book, *Identity and the Life Cycle*, he emphasizes that integrity may represent the culmination of all the preceding stages. In this last lap around the track, we can draw upon Erikson's understanding that our lives, all our choices, the weight of fate, and our attitude about all these things, will be driven by integrity, or the search for depth and new meaning. Erikson writes, "Only he who in some way has taken care of things and people and has adapted himself to the triumphs and disappointments of being, by necessity the originator of others and generator of things and ideas—only he may gradually grow the fruit of these (prior) stages. I know no better word for it than ego integrity."[85] This is Erikson's way of highlighting that in the sunset in life, one may come to a sense of peace and satisfaction about one's worth, one's past, and one's future. Is this the counter-narrative to despair? It seems appropriate to note that some accept ego integrity as the heritage they've created for themselves, while others languish in the despair of missed opportunities or misspent possibilities.

The signs of ego integrity may be marked by the fact that we have sought and received guidance from someone of strong regard in our past. These highly regarded individuals may be the fruit of a long-lasting relationship from an earlier stage of adulthood, likely someone we might call a mentor. For some of us, the person could be a parent or a grandparent or even someone with whom we have shared a reciprocal relationship of importance. The idea of reciprocity is a strong theme for older adults, who relate to our important, younger friends even as we become mentors for them.

A second sign of ego integrity is a heightened concern for the world, a widened perspective that includes our embrace of others whom we may not even know. This level of integrity includes attitudes of maturity such as tolerance, patience, compassion, and open-mindedness. It can be marked as the ability to recognize both sides of a complicated issue and refusing to collapse an issue to a one-sided, simplistic understanding.

Another characteristic of the development of ego integrity is our awareness that we must embrace a newer philosophy of aging. The narrow assumptions from the point of view of those who have not reached this age must be challenged so we can continue to seek purpose in order to avoid stagnation in older adulthood. People who do this with purpose continue to maintain a positive daily routine and also maintain positive relationships with others. People of integrity infuse these positive traits with a sense of humor about others and themselves.

A fourth characteristic of ego integrity is that we may come to new conclusions about our faith or the lack thereof. Many of us renew ourselves to a deeper, more meaningful relationship with what we call "God." This is a non-sectarian observation and may be true of any who find themselves more curious about God, about the meaning of their lives, and about the future with all its mysteries. We may connect more intimately to the religion of our childhood, or we may even connect to a faith that is more appropriate to our lives in this older adult stage. Our renewed faith may or may not result in returning to a particular faith community, and it may be marked by a new affirmation of personal spirituality.

While only a recent citizen of this older adulthood stage myself, I watched both of my parents as they lived through this stage until the end. Both of them found ways to deepen their conversation of partnership with one another. They became more dependent on one another, but both of them viewed that dependence as a sign of their mutual commitment. In fine-tuning their relationship, they were making their vows to one another concrete and meaningful. Even in their physical decline, they were both students of life through reading, always with books by the nightstand, and by their frequent visits to the small-town library that was a center of the community's cultural life. They were known by the library employees and volunteered on occasion to support the learning events there. My father served on the library board and used his artistic creativity to design a monthly front cover for the library newsletter. He and the head librarian developed monthly themes that my father would then illustrate. Perhaps no one in town had an appreciative thought about any of this, but it was important to my father. He was such a reader that he noted in one of his many letters that he had "read the library out," meaning he had read just about everything he had an interest in reading, maybe not all the books but certainly the ones he deemed worth reading.

My father was an advertising designer, a commercial artist in his work life. But as he aged, he returned to the drawing board and went back to his original life as an expressive artist. He dabbled in oils but spent most of his time teaching himself the fine arts of watercolors and pen and ink drawings. He sketched and created working models of pieces he wanted to complete. He allowed that his art was a way of seeing the world, and he wanted it to present his point of view of the simple things that make life rich.

Upon his death a few years after our mother died, we observed the ritual of dividing his many artworks between us. We determined how the lottery would be agreed upon, and once we created an order of choosing, all choices were evenly made. We assembled all the artwork in my parents' large living room, leaning each piece against the walls in a massive exhibition. There were paintings from art school and a few three-dimensional pieces made for other purposes. There were ample numbers of watercolors and pen and ink drawings. Many were already framed, but some were not. Since our mother had died three years earlier, this lottery of artwork was part of a larger distribution of their remaining possessions. This was a final act of making decisions of what to keep, what to sell, and what to give away. For three sons who had grown up in this home, our choices were an essential part of the grieving process. It was an acknowledgment that we had indeed "moved up in line," as we were now the elders of the family our parents had brought into being.

We discovered a few surprises in going through every drawer, every closet, and every box. There were photographs that spanned nearly a century or more. The oldest photographs included relatives we could no longer identify. We soon recognized our mother was the resident memory for the family, and now our keeper of the family history was no longer available to help us understand who these people were or what role they played in the family tree. Even today, I have one of those early photographs from sometime in the nineteenth century, picturing a forefather I cannot name. No one seems to know who he is with any specificity. Beyond us, there are no other sources we can ask, as all our parents are deceased. We think this bearded ancient daguerreotype photograph may depict our maternal grandmother's family, perhaps even her grandfather on her mother's side, but who knows for sure?

One surprise in the paperwork from our mother's early adulthood was a note of her desire to go to college. She had dreams and she had plans, but those plans were interrupted by the war, the pragmatics of finding work after high school to support herself, and eventually the task of being mother to a toddler and an infant in the span of a year while trying to juggle work and the demands of home. That which she desired went unfulfilled, but never did we hear a complaint or even an acknowledgment of these dreams. All of this was revealed by going through the leftovers of the boxes holding a lifetime of dreams. It deepened what we knew about our parents, as if we were archaeologists to a couple who lived across the arc of their lives, and all that remained was contained in the boxes and in the scattered storage containers.

Between the three of us, our differences in personality were revealed in how we considered keeping or getting rid of our parents' many things. Most of my decisions about choosing things for myself were informed by the pragmatic limitation of what would fit into my car for the 600-mile drive home. I made the decision that I would not haul a trailer that far, so I chose smaller things. My two brothers lived nearby. In the end, we had to decide how to best get rid of the things we did not want for ourselves, and multiple trips were made to the local auction shop where online shoppers could bid pennies on the dollar for groupings of items.

Is this how it is done? Is this how all of our lives will be remembered? Will our families fight over our things, or do we even have anything worth fighting over? In the final handful of years as our parents aged, we three sons made value statements in advance to shape how we would go through this last stage together. We determined that we would not allow anything to get between us and that our relationships with each other represented an enduring value we wanted to save. We sought to be honest and fair to one another as an extension of what our parents had taught us all our lives. We lifted up these thoughts in advance as guiding statements that helped us witness to our love for one another. That shared sense of identity was a distinct part of our upbringing, and now we could choose to live out those values in our ongoing relationship with one another. That certitude and intentionality remain with us today.

People of integrity are often able to come to a peaceful acceptance of the life they have lived, acknowledging and accepting their past choices. Everyone has a past, and that past is made by making choices. There are ongoing issues that likely mark one's current life, and those choices may be sustained in the memory as regret and shame. Regardless, this last stage of personal maturity means we are aware of the past and may make new choices that deal with the leftovers of earlier stages. If we are successful in dealing with our past, a conversion may take place that allows a fresh start even into this final stage of life.

The earlier essay on childhood highlighted the series of "firsts" children face. At the beginning, a child has one first after another. Children necessarily face each first in striking out on the journey of life. "There's a first time for everything," we say, and in the beginning, everything is a first. Then the child begins to depend on the regularity they can assume after the first has been tried and accomplished. Going forward, the child can trust that it is possible again and again.

And so it goes across the arc of life, until we surely face that there will be a series of "lasts." A last time driving a car. A last time cooking our own meal or cleaning our own house. A last time to walk down the street. A last round of golf. A last trip to the grocery store to buy our own food. A last time to make love with our partner or lover in life. A last time to leave our house and all we possess after a lifetime of collecting our own furniture, books, hobbies, and everything else we might own. These "lasts" mirror a child's firsts in almost every detail.

In coming to the end of the arc of life, we discover we've been preparing for this most of our lives, whether we understood what we were doing or not. After all, interconnectedness permeates all of life. We come to see that childhood is interwoven into adolescence, and adolescence is interwoven into adulthood, and all the stages in life are interconnected to the other stages almost in a seamless whole rather than a series of disjointed experiences. Each part of life is connected to the whole of it, and so the end is connected to the beginning. Charles Dickens observed, "As I draw closer and closer to the end, I travel in a circle nearer and nearer to the beginning."[86] We may come to realize, as Claypool describes it, "What we are to be in the future we are now becoming."[87] The old saying is true: "We become more and more what we already are." We live through most of it having little or no insight into this truth, but toward the end we achieve the wisdom to see it.

In fact, we've been laying the foundations for this last stage since childhood because of the vast interconnectedness of life. This idea was voiced in the first pages of this collection of essays: "The stories appear to be linear, one after the other, but at the same time they are cyclical, and the cycle of stories is commonly experienced by others whose stories are intersected. Linear life events, one after another, can purposefully take us from our beginnings, meander through the middleness of life, and come back to merge with one's endings." Wisdom is gained by living in acceptance of these claims.

We may be consumed with the worries that have accumulated across the arc of life. Such worries may include financial security as our opportunities to support ourselves financially have shriveled, and an accounting of how we have prepared for this stage will be evident. Perhaps we worry about unfinished agendas or about mistakes whose effects linger. Almost certainly, we worry about our diminished physical capacities or illness, or we struggle with the fear of the loss of cognition and the escape from memory or awareness. We watch as our friends and others who are dear to us die, and it seems all we do is attend funerals. The limitations in life mount up, and there's little to be done about these losses. In response, we may grow tender about it, or we may become angry. This is the shadowed journey, and we are forced to the point of acceptance even when we cannot tolerate it.

There is, then, an odd syncopation to this age as we ask, Is it *more* or is it *less*? We have more free time to do whatever we want to do, yet we live knowing the shot clock is winding down. We sport more wrinkles on our translucent skin and may be perpetually, incessantly bruised, yet we discover vanity is a waste of time and learn to give little thought to how our skin tells our stories for us. Our social life is structured around doctor visits, and our bathroom cabinets are littered by uncountable medications. We are limited by diet restrictions meant not just for our BMI but also for our internal organs and the fragile balance of our body's chemistry. More than ever, we are like the walking wounded with all our aches and pains, and, unlike at any other time, we are threatened by our balance, needing to be aware of our stability when we're on our feet. Our reactions are slow to nearly nonresponsive, so anytime we tilt, we may fall. And if we fall (something known as "the event" in our household), we are perilously close to that moment when our lives are on the verge of changing suddenly and irreversibly. The "event," whatever it might be, may be a crisis of existence with the power to disrupt our mobility, our freedom, our cognition, even our very lives.

Thankfully, in this last stage we also have a deep appreciation for our friends and our family, and yet ironically we may be lonelier than at any other time as we slowly lose our friends, our neighbors, our loves. We watch in futility as life ends for key figures in our lives, and there are empty spaces in our hearts and minds where there was once a person dear to us who is no longer here. Our loneliness may feel despairing in our time of need.

We come to a point where we are driven by our opinions, which are many. We are obsessed by them, and they may increase our loneliness as those around us step away from the strident and isolated views that we hold as nonnegotiable truths. We are attracted to strident opinionators whose purpose seem to be to unleash fear and anxiety as a generational weapon of destruction.

This last stage, the seventh decade and beyond, is open-ended until closer inspection. It's open-ended because there is no other stage beyond it. For some, it's a gateway period that closes quickly, almost too soon, we might feel. For some, the end can't come soon enough as they are traveling on through life and discover they're on a cul-de-sac where the journey plays itself out. Death can be a long, slow decline as though it is not in a hurry. "To everything, there is a season," the wisdom poet writes (Eccl 3:8, NRSV). But before death comes, what life is being lived? How do we embrace this last stage for the possible richness it holds out to us?

In her studies of terminally ill patients, psychiatrist Dr. Elisabeth Kübler-Ross speculated that the dying go through five distinct stages of grief preceding their deaths (denial, anger, bargaining, depression, and acceptance). Those studies produced a book titled *On Death and Dying*[88] that brought the forbidden topic of terminal illness into public discourse. The result was the development of hospice care as a means to care for patients in their dying days with dignity.

Just a few years ago, Dr. Kübler-Ross herself died after her own bout with cancer. Her son observed, "For her, death wasn't something to fear. It was like a graduation." Kübler-Ross moved to Arizona in the mid-1990s after a series of strokes left her partially paralyzed. She lived ready for death. In a 2002 interview with *The Arizona Republic*, she said she was ready to die: "I told God last night he's a damned procrastinator." As she grew ever closer to her death, she continued to enjoy her few satisfying habits of smoking cigarettes, eating Swiss chocolates, and shopping. Toward the end, she described her impending death: "Death is simply a shedding of the physical body like the butterfly shedding its cocoon. It is a transition to a higher state of consciousness where you continue to perceive, to understand, to laugh, and to be able to grow."[89]

Dennis Klass, her former research assistant, observed, "That soft-spoken, iron-willed, sometimes crazy, interpersonal, little woman went around the world and changed the way people thought about themselves and their families and how they thought about life and death." Awaiting death was not such a challenge for her, her son reported. He said, "Her only problem with facing death was patience. She was looking forward to dancing with the stars."

For some, the richness of life can extend for many years, and while one may accommodate major life shifts, the experience of a fully lived life can be a long sunset with many colors and beauties yet to enjoy. Thus we measure this stage as the seventh decade *and beyond.* That "beyond" offers lower expectations for life, but it can go for some time when one is still living independently, still growing, still alive with purpose.

Religion and theology do not represent answers as much as they stand at the border between time and eternity and bear witness with metaphors, stories, and poetry regarding things about which we can say no more with any assured finality. In his old age, Einstein was asked what he thought about life after death. He remarked that he did not know any more than anyone else might know, but it was enough to have gotten a glimpse. What is ahead, he noted, is likely too great to imagine, certainly too much for words. Perhaps it's enough for any of us simply to get a glimpse.

Story Starters–Older Adulthood

• **Leftovers from Middle Adulthood.** For many, leaving middle adulthood is a reckoning of sorts, as there is likely some unfinished business. What does it mean that an expectation goes unfulfilled? For some, this can be a bittersweet feeling, a longing for more time, a realization that time has run short. What shifts in our thinking are required so we can cling to hope as the next stage emerges? How have you marked this moment of recognition?

• **Social Life.** Social life for older adults can be vibrant if they are able to seek new friends and recognize opportunities to embrace new interests. At this stage, we now have time for the social life we've always wanted but couldn't pursue due to busyness. What stories can you tell about pursuing these new interests?

• **Friends.** The joy of long-term friendships can diminish as we lose these friends through death or disability. We must nurture new friends in order to keep up with the losses. Tender friendships are more precious than gold. To find companionship through a shared life can be deep and meaningful. Upon losing such a friend, one may enter a stage of despair and sorrow. Share a story of friendship to explore how you experienced the companionship of another person as a meaningful sense of community.

• **Failure and Loss.** No one gets through life without scars from experiences gone bad. This last stage of adulthood can be a rich occasion that Richard Rohr calls "falling up." How have your failures, while painful at the time, turned out to be rewards leading you to a deeper way of life? How have those failures or losses given you a new perspective on life or on others? While no one wants to relive such experiences by repeating them, have the values gained outweighed the losses?

• **Life Partners/Marriage.** Many people find companionship for their journey through life. Companions are people we identify as partners in life who can travel the journey with us and share with us all that life has to offer. Some of those relationships result in marriage, and in others people have made deep and long-lasting commitments to one another. Most marriages are marked by rituals such as the exchange of rings and the affirmation of vows. How have you continued to demonstrate these commitments in ritual ways? When these relationships break up or one of the partners dies, how are those disruptions experienced in ritual form? We are typically young and inexperienced in the season when we choose partners for life. What wisdom did you use in making your commitment to the one you loved? Looking back, did you have what you needed to make this choice? Do you have second thoughts? Any regrets? Wish you could have a "do over"? In this stage, many lose their life partner to death. If this has happened to you, how have you coped in moving forward?

• **Career and Vocation.** For many, this topic is simply called "work," needing no deeper term of description. But for others, work turns into a career or even a vocation. What term do you use to describe the life path you have taken to serve you and those you love with resources that come in response to your spent energies? If you choose *work*, what does that mean to you? If you choose *career* or *vocation*, why did you choose those terms? When did *work* turn into a *career* or a *vocation*? What about second chances? Do you have thoughts on "the path not taken"? Do you have regrets about not pursuing a different path?

• **Identity.** On this end of the arc of life, how do you regard your identity as a person? How do others see you? How do you see yourself? Is your self-identity what you hoped it would be? Are you driven by actions or by values? How do these aspects inform your sense of self? We tend to equate our identity with our accomplishments. Do you have a sense of self that is *not driven* by your accomplishments?

• **Forgiveness and Reconciliation.** What relational issues of forgiveness do you need to resolve in this last stage of adulthood? What action, what conversation, what move needs to be made to initiate reconciliation? How long have you carried this burden, and how willing are you to take the action that may bring about reconciliation?

• **God.** Across the arc of life, we have different understandings of God, of faith, of religious belief. Some have lived according to a religious tradition, while others have lived apart from any tradition of faith. How does your chosen view represent your deepest yearnings about life? Does being in the last stage of adulthood have any bearing on how you answer these questions?

Journal

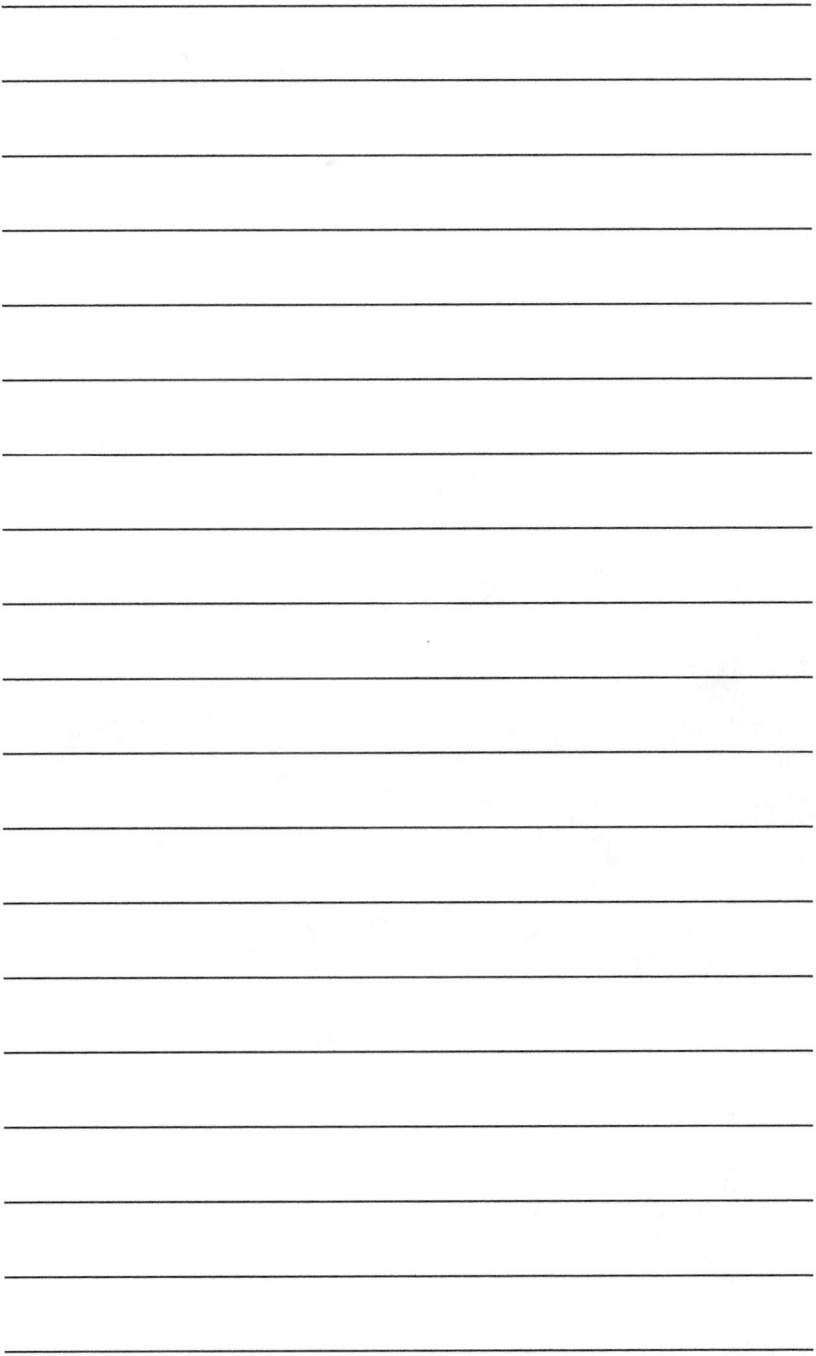

Epilogue Stories– How Your Story Continues

The journey across the arc of life from childhood to older adulthood begins with dependence. Then, as growth and maturity occur, the journey moves decidedly to independence. To regain balance, one wisely mediates to interdependence and back to dependence in the last stage, which forms an arc for how each person is connected to others. The arc of life bends through all these stages until it resembles the dependence of one's beginning, utterly dependent on others for life to exist. Even John, the friend of Jesus, was prophetically told that he would not die prematurely as many did in his time, implying that he would die at the conclusion of his own arc. But his prophecy came with a terrible truth: "Very truly, I tell you when you were younger, you used to fasten your own belt and go wherever wished. But when you grow old, you will stretch out your hands, and someone else will fasten a belt around you and take you where you do not wish to go" (John 21:18, NRSV).

All of this is typical, even normal, unless life is interrupted by an illness, an accident, or one of the other countless reasons life comes to an end. Plainly, some do not live across a full-orbed arc. They are the ones whose journey is interrupted, cut short from the full span of life. But many do make the journey all the way to the end, when their existence is claimed by the architect of life. "To everything, there is a season," the wisdom poet writes (Eccl 3:8, NRSV), despite our inclination to challenge this wisdom. Some die all too soon; others linger painfully, praying for death to come and take them. It's a journey everyone makes, all who have come to completion and have stepped across the threshold of life into death.

The final journey may be considered tragic for some or a blessed relief for others. But does that mark the end? Or does the arc of life continue forward past death, sustained by others who bear bits and pieces of us? Do others keep our stories alive? How long do the reverberations continue? Few life stories have lasting presence in the generations that follow. Admittedly, there are a few people whose lives continue to draw our attention. For such individuals, the light shone so brightly in life that it still glows after death, sustained in others who continue to view them as either an aspirational legacy or covered in utter shame. For others, the light shone well on life, and that light may continue to shine for some time for a generation or two. For most, the light has only a faint glow in family or close friends, but it will surely diminish with the death of each person who had a front row seat to your story. If death does not define the end of the arc of one's life, what meaning does that give to those who are exploring their own stories? How is life's meaning understood to extend beyond one's existence? Can one embrace the full journey even through decline and death and beyond to see that life's echoes will continue on in the lives of others?

Everyone's journey is different, and there are an unending number of ways a person's path can go in its own direction. Life itself, perhaps even what I have called "the contract of life," demands that we must follow our own paths as they appear to us. The end and the beginning are amazingly near to one another; the arc reminds us of the cyclical nature of time. There's a birth and there's a death. From alpha to omega, from beginning to end, it varies from person to person, but the pathway's outcome is virtually the same in result. Only the details differ. Many do not want to face the reality of decline and death, but it is written into the design, part of the contract of life, that life follows a cycle "all the way to the end." Our end is certain no matter how hard the mystics argue.

These truths are well trod by artists, writers, poets, and authors when they follow the Greek philosopher's narrative framework that every story has a beginning, a middle, and an end. Aristotle's view is the mainframe for telling a story. It's how we see all of life. It's the way dramatists portray the world. It's how little children tell their first story of an adventure or experience they've had. "Tell me your story" is an invitation to build your tale around these three movements. We may not tell the whole story, but we typically fragment it into smaller episodes, vignettes, all of which are bits and pieces of the whole.

If there is a prologue to the stories we joined at our birth, there is also an epilogue for how our stories continue past our deaths. Our stories don't begin in the instance of birth, and they don't end at the moment of death. The river analogy suggests that prologue stories are "upriver" and epilogue stories are "downriver" of a lived life. For a while, the stories of our lives go on beyond our living in the minds and memories of those we have loved before disappearing like all memories do, with very few exceptions. Like the continuing reverberations of the gong of the bell, an echo of your life continues, pulsating with strength at first but then eventually dying out. First with the deaths of our elders, our grandparents, and later at the deaths of our parents, we can see how those important figures are yet still with us. Each generation that follows is no better than a half-life in memory from those who have died. Two generations away would be half of that, likely no more, until almost no tangible memories exist other than a genealogical record and a handful of photographs to frame our memories in frozen moments. What happens to their stories? What is remembered about their dreams, their friends, their adventures, their personal sorrows and losses? How does the arc of their lives live on if there is no memory of it? "All rivers run to the sea," we hear. Do their stories go to the sea where all others go, held in its blue depths? Is there an ocean of memory that waters the lowest places on the earth? Jung imagined a collective unconscious where such universally shared memories are gathered. It's a mystical belief to be sure, almost eastern by nature, but is this where all things go? Is there a place where all unremembered memories continue to exist and are stored, each one totally unique but in kind with others as a fulfillment of the human story?

No matter. All such memories, remembered or not, are carried on the river of time. The ancients measured time in two ways. One way is in the sequence of day that follows day, one after another, marching along in an endless procession. In order to measure time sequentially, we count the days. We create units of measurement so we can keep them organized: seconds, hours, days, weeks, months, years, centuries, millennia, and infinite eons beyond. A stopwatch can fragment even a single second. A daily calendar can and will slide into the history books. The keeping of time's minutiae is never ending, like the waves of the sea, one wave after another in a parade breaking on the shores of the world. Tick tock, tick tock. Scientists are delving into time's ever-flowing beginnings, marching up the stream to the headwaters where all existence began in a flash of such power that time and matter were both launched.

Clearly our perceptions of time evolve as we go from one stage to another across the arc of life until we come to the conclusion that the shot clock is running to zero. In our last stage of adulthood, we see time as the commodity it is and as diminishing capital, moving at an ever-increasing pace as it runs its course.[90] All the while, our productivity goes down (or slows down) while our meaning increases. It is critical to our internal self-appreciation that we locate our lives in meaning. Paul Tournier helps us claim our happiness, saying that true happiness is linked with deep, inner harmony. This kind of harmony is likely not an accident but the result of a lifetime of preparation.[91] In the metaphor of the steward, these are the fruits gleaned from the seeds we cast broadly into the world. Some seeds are cast with intent, while others are serendipitous, almost as if by accident, certainly the kind that are sown by a generous hand in the world. There is great mystery in all this, perhaps evidence of a larger intent that governs the universe.

But the ancients also reckoned that time was cyclical, following the seasons: one season after another in a never-ending cycle of time. One season is born, lives, and gives way to another season in an endless cycle that repeats itself over and over and over again. In either way of measuring time, whether we see it strictly as a sequence or accept that we are buoyed along on rolling cycles of time, we recognize that our life's arc has a beginning, a middle, and an end, from beginning to end and back to the beginning, we say. Is time sequential or is it cyclical? Clearly, it's both. These two ways of seeing time give us a chance of viewing life as moving forward moment by moment, across the arc of time.

Try this experiment: Lie as still as you can, take several deep breaths to calm yourself, and still your anxious thoughts to the point that you are as stopped from all motion as possible. Quiet your thoughts as best you can. Feel the stillness? Feel as though the world has stopped spinning? Even if you were stone cold dead, you would still be a body in motion. No matter how successful you are in stopping your world, it's a deception because the world is constantly in motion in ways we cannot even conceive. Specifically, did you know that even if you are as still as a rock on the ground, despite that apparent stillness, you are spinning at over 1,000 miles per hour? It's all a matter of science and math, as the Earth rotates once every 23 hours, 56 minutes, and 4.09053 seconds, and since the circumference of the Earth is roughly 40,075 kilometers, the surface of the Earth at the equator moves at a speed of 460 meters per second. That is based on the speed of the Earth's rotation at the equator. Convert the metrics to Imperial units, and we arrive at a round number of 1,000 mph. Either way, we don't feel the Earth's rotation or spin because we're all moving with it, at the same constant speed.

One more layer of truth about motion: the Earth "circles" the sun at a speed of nearly 67,000 mph. To be technical, this orbit is not perfectly circular but is elliptical depending on the gravitational pull of the other bodies also in motion in their own orbits. It's more of the same: we calculate that the Earth is moving around our sun in a circular orbit, covering this route at a speed of nearly 30 kilometers per second or 67,000 miles per hour. What does the sun spin around, and at what speed? Scientists figure that the solar system is traveling at an average speed of 828,000 km/h or 514,000 mph within its trajectory around the galactic center, a speed at which an object could circumnavigate the Earth's equator in 2 minutes and 54 seconds. That speed corresponds to approximately one 1300th of the speed of light. The galactic year, also known as a cosmic year, is the duration of time required for the solar system to orbit once around the center of the Milky Way Galaxy. Estimates range from 225 to 250 million terrestrial years.

Are you still lying on the floor? The cosmic highway patrol would pull you over for excessive speeding if they could catch you. The ancients had no notion of this cosmic motion, but they understood the essentials of the power of time, one moment after another, and of the turning of the seasons. They understood the simple truth that life has a beginning, a middle, and an end.

On another level, take that motionless, lifeless rock on the ground. You can't see it, but at the atomic level, there is subatomic motion happening in each and every atom. It may look as though the rock is absolutely still, but in truth it is a beehive of activity as the subatomic materials are spinning at speeds our brains cannot comprehend. The electrons, protons, and neutrons (not to mention the other subatomic particles—quarks, gluons, photons, muons, pions, kaons, and neutrinos, etc.) are spinning so fast it's amazing we don't fall down and quiver like a blob of Jell-O. The study of subatomic particles is called particle physics. These particles are often held together within an atom by one of the four fundamental forces (gravity, electromagnetic force, strong force, or weak force). Outside of the atom, the particles move near the speed of light, which is its own definition of speed, or at least the calculus for measuring immense distances in space. Even beyond that, the hardness of the rock is a total misconception; it is mostly void, for each atom is as empty as outer space itself, with the emptiness created between the subatomic materials. It's more like outer space, with a few rocks thrown out in the midst of the void to make it all interesting.

In the end, what remains? What are the leftovers from your lifetime's journey? When you reach the end of your life, and you are buried and gone, what of you will continue? Will you be missed? How will those who survive hold their memory of you? What residue of habits or thinking or values or shame will be held in memory? Likely, we will at last be released from all of those burdens.

After we have crossed the arc of life and come to the end, what part of us remains? Or do we simply fade into a lost past where no shred of us exists? Playwright, actor, and director Nöel Coward's poem "Nothing Is Lost" was originally titled "What's Going to Happen to the Children?" when he wrote it back in 1927. As he reflects on the question, "What remains after one's life comes to completion?" Easily, we can recognize the innumerable influence of ideas, thoughts, and emotions that others have had on our lives, leaving an indelible mark.

> Deep in our sub-conscious, we are told
> Lie all our memories, lie all the notes
> Of all the music we have ever heard
> And all the phrases those we loved have spoken [. . .][92]

The question of whether there are residual effects showing that we have lived, have experienced all that life has presented with courage and diligence, and have left some mark on those around us or on a community of peers is honest and boundless. Ringing the gong leaves an ongoing vibration of sound long after it has been struck, but eventually those vibrations are stilled and the gong is finally silent. What might we expect beyond those things we know to be true? The wheels of time turn steadily forward, and our mark on the world is limited. The ancient Hebrew poet was truthful:

> Lord, you have been our dwelling place in all generations.
> Before the mountains were brought forth,
> Or ever you had formed the earth and the world,
> From everlasting to everlasting you are God.
> You turn us back to dust . . .
> For a thousand years in your sight are like yesterday when it is past,
> Or like a watch in the night.
> You sweep them away; they are like a dream,
> Like grass that is renewed in the morning;

In the morning it flourishes and is renewed;
In the evening it fades and withers. (Ps 90:1-5, NRSV)[93]

This wisdom of the ancients was true in its day, and nothing has changed that truth. How would we ever know how our lives are like the gong that has been rung?

In her startling book *For the Time Being*, writer Annie Dillard cites an amazing discovery by anthropologist Mary Leakey on the dry Laetoli plains of northern Tanzania. It was there that Leakey found a trail of hominid footprints. There were three barefoot people—likely a short man, woman, and child *Australopithecus*—who walked closely together, perhaps as a family. The three ancients walked on moist volcanic tuff and ash, leaving behind a brief record from a single day about 3.6 million years ago. The dating of these steps comes before hominids even chipped stone tools. The day was captured as more ash covered the footprints and subsequently hardened. The ash was so effective in this record that it even preserved the pockmarks of the raindrops that fell beside the three who walked. Almost ninety feet of the footprints were preserved. What we don't know is significant, leaving the gaps as questions. We do not know where they were going or why. We do not know why the woman paused and turned left, briefly, before continuing. "A remote ancestor," Leakey surmised, "experienced a moment of doubt." Possibly she turned to watch the Sadiman volcano erupting, as may have been happening at the time, or for some reason maybe she took a last look back. Annie Dillard's comments on the footsteps are alive with meaning for us today: "We do not know nor can we make anything so lasting as these three barefoot ones did."[94] Dillard's book is about the weight of time, something that gives us pause as we take our arc of life and place it alongside the length and width of a story so immense as to be fabled. We are humbled by the speck of time that we inhabit and call our own. The string of lives that are described in our prologue stories are also immense, and many spend significant portions of their middle and older adulthood researching the trace lines of everyone who lives upstream from our own lives. We can also turn our focus downstream to the future lives that may be as curious about us as we are about those before us.

What do we leave behind? What lasting memories are made because we lived? What impact do we make, good or bad, on those around us? What memories of us will survive more than a generation or two? The remains come in waves. First, there's the obvious, the physical remains that are passed along to children through DNA and, likely, the habits of being.

Children whose biological parents are active in their lives can benefit from the long-term health history of those parents. Children who are adopted may not have the benefit of their health history and may be disconnected from that genetic knowledge. (Fortunately, almost half the states now allow adoptees some access to health histories or other records that can help them discover genetic information.) Over the long course of time, that kind of history is often of great value as the child grows. But there's more. One's habits of being are typically ingrained values that come from lessons taught and life lessons lived as examples from our family and other significant mentors. For those closest to us, the lessons can be both positive and negative as we live authentically and fully.

My grandfather died just after Christmas during my sophomore year of college. He was considered the patriarchal figure on my mother's side of the family. He was a centralizing character in my life, and all of us in my mother's family were in some orbit created by him and featured some aspect of his spirit. He was a constant source of fun and wisdom, and, as he lived to retirement, he continued to cast a long shadow across us all. I was off at school, but I felt strongly connected to him despite the distance. My grandmother was equally a matriarchal figure with many of the same characteristics although he was the sun and she was the moon. We were all stars in their universe.

Three days after Christmas, he fell gravely ill and died early the next morning. My younger brother, who was only eleven years old, was with our grandfather when our he collapsed with what we learned later was a blood clot. We had no warning, nor were we prepared for the hole that was left in our worlds. I watched my mother grieve while caring for us as a family. I watched my grandmother, the daily source of strength and resolve for me as I grew up, rise and stand strong while also grieving her own deep sense of loss. Likewise, my sister-cousin and her parents were stung by this news. My older brother and I and our sister-cousin all returned to college the following week. However, over the years, I've learned to see this tragedy through the eyes of my younger brother, who provided the first response to his fall. He had to muster the next steps of how to call our grandmother, who could call for the ambulance and begin calling her daughter (our mother) and her son (our uncle) to respond. This is my younger brother's story of having to face his fear and to know that he had to do something in order to ring the bell on our grandfather's behalf.

My grandfather's death forced us to recalibrate our family system in the absence of a centralizing father figure. His absence was a form of painful presence. His chair in which we sat only in respectful awe was now empty. His place at the table was vacant; his ever-present word of wisdom was now silent; his laugh and his way of seeing the world through old rural eyes were gone. The strength of the family was based on the love and care of both grandparents, and because of that, the family regrouped.

My grandmother lived another twenty-five years, into her nineties. She held my grandfather's presence as treasured memories in the years after his death. She was our token physical reminder of his great light. She was a steady source of life on her own, but part of holding his memory was contained in her own being. One day in her late eighties, she and I were at the sink washing and drying the dishes from a meal we had all shared. I asked her a blunt and simple question: "Do you miss him?" I did not have to name him for the question to make sense, as we both understood. I would not have dared to ask such a probing question of any other octogenarian who had lost her long-loved husband of half a century, but I knew I could ask my grandmother because we shared deep love and honesty. I was stunned at how silent she became and at the tears that welled up in her eyes. She said simply, "I miss him a lot."

She helped give words to my own deep sense of grief over his absence. I missed him in my own way but was humbled by the depth of her memory. In that moment, I was borrowing from her words and tears for my own need. Is this the way it is in families where death removes a significant figure around whom the whole family is built? Perhaps some families experience the same kind of emptiness due to the lack of such a person to hold it all together, but in families like mine, the absence speaks loudly, not filling the place that was previously held by their life, their spirit, their abiding sense of wholeness.

Earlier, I recalled a day of walking through the Cottage Hill Cemetery outside of Celina, just north of Dallas, and thought about seeing the rich reminders of my family members who had joined the others in their deaths as a community of memory and identity. My grandfather was there, but my grandmother took another generation to join him. My aunts and uncles from the wider range of our family have also joined them. But now this cemetery is nearly complete with the addition of my sister-cousin's parents, my aunt and uncle, and also with my own parents, who all died within a few years of one another in their mid-eighties.

The family has continued to grow, however, and is bigger now than it was a generation ago. The generation of my nephews and niece, my sister-cousin's son, and our own two kids now inhabits a layer of family that has filled in nicely to replace the positions taken by the generation just above mine. Is this the cycle of life that keeps turning? My brothers and I observed at our father's death that we all moved up in line; now we are the elders of our family system. The three sons and the sister-cousin are all keeping the family identity coherent and life-giving. We are the holders of the family memory, even though the family historian (my mother) died, and with her went much of the family history that we can no longer recite. The graveyard has been filled, and the dead of the future will likely need to expand to another location. How will the family consider a new physical site for us to gather? This question has no answer, and it will be one of the challenges we face in the epilogue years. It is taking nearly a decade for us to answer these questions of how the family will sustain itself.

Bringing us all together (unless it's for a funeral) has become more of a challenge than ever before, whereas in our childhood the family lived in two counties, no more than half an hour apart. Today, we live across the South and the Midwest, and there's always the chance that one of our kids will launch to who knows where. What value does geographical proximity play in helping us get together? No longer do we load up our own children at Thanksgiving or Christmas to make a family trip to be with all the cousins, as our kids are just as busy as their cousins. The time spent together is more fragmented than ever, so how will these younger people know their full identity with such scraps from the family table? Every generation goes through these issues, and there are no firm solutions here to improve how families might face them together. When I think about my elder family members, I see that the younger generation has so little clue about them that they don't matter now. In truth, they will learn who they are as members of this family from us, who learned it from our elders. We are the elders now, and our task is to make sure the identity is passed along in ways that will sustain and nurture them. The cycle of life is made real every time we gather for a meal or a cookout or a holiday weekend together. The richness of creating memories and making connections to all with whom we share life is not an accident; it is an intentional effort meant to give life to those in our immediate circle of generations.

That's only a small portion of how our lives and our stories continue. The leftover material of our lives is vast and largely unreported. Some is understood consciously, while most of it is beyond our naming and a part of the unconscious memory. What of your story, bits and pieces of your lived experience, will survive? From beginning to end, the rituals of our lives shape each hour, day, and year. Everyone leads a ritualized life. Rituals are repeated patterns of meaningful acts. If you are mindful of your actions, you will see the ritual patterns. If you see the patterns, you may understand them. If you understand them, you may enrich them. In this way, the habits of a lifetime become sacred.[95]

Story Starters–Epilogue Stories

• **Possessions.** If you could be intentional about the material things associated with your life after your death, how would you identify those things, and, better yet, how would you transfer them with intentionality? How would you pass them along to those you love? How would you see that these things were carried by those with whom you entrusted them? Will your family value your things in the same way you have valued them? What non-material possessions do you wish to offer? How will you intentionally pass them along?

• **Death Stories.** Are there any ongoing stories or themes in your family? How has your family used rituals to mark the deaths of family members? How do you imagine your family will account for your absence after your death? What rituals might be observed at your dying? For, as F. Forrester Church writes, "All of us die in the middle of our story."[96]

• **Regret.** There are usually leftovers of unresolved issues that remain after we die. These unresolved leftovers could be business that was not completed, a relationship that has fractured, or a turn in the road not taken. How have you experienced regret, and what have been the long-term results of that regret?

• **Lament.** What deep feelings of loss have been expressed at family funerals?

• **Forgiveness and Reconciliation.** Is there a story of pain or wrong running through your epilogue stories? Knowing this, is there anything you want to do to resolve it?

• **Expectations/Disappointment at Your Death.** Have you come to understand how your passing will be celebrated and how your death will be a struggle for your family? What expectations, spoken and unspoken, have been placed upon your passing? What disappointments might be identified about you upon your death? What stories do you want shared at your funeral? What stories would you rather not be shared? Would you consider letting others share them with your family or friends either before or after your funeral?

• **Rituals.** How does your family observe rituals in their life together at someone's death? How does the family mark significant events such as the loss of someone in your family? Death occurs with community rituals: death watch, announcement of death, family visitation, funeral or memorial service, committal of bodily remains (casket) or ashes (urn), etc. What will your family do at your death? If you could coach them about the rituals you prefer, what would you suggest? What do you like about these rituals? What do you not like?

• **Social Life.** How do you expect your friends will think about your death? What might they say to each other when they gather at your funeral?

• **God/Faith.** How is faith present in your stories? How is faith present in the lives of the people who will remain upon your death? Is there a faith tradition you have joined? Is it still present in your life? What God stories can be told from these traditions? What thoughts about the soul shape your belief in God, in eternity, in heaven or hell, in life evermore?

• **Acceptance.** What agreements have you made in your life you think might continue on? What strengths are evident? What limitations have you faced?

• **Inheritance.** What was left to you when your parents died? Did your parents indicate specifically what you should receive, or did you have to devise a system to make those decisions? How did you and any siblings you have divide things up? What is the difference between an inheritance and a legacy? Do you see the importance of both for those you leave behind?

Journal

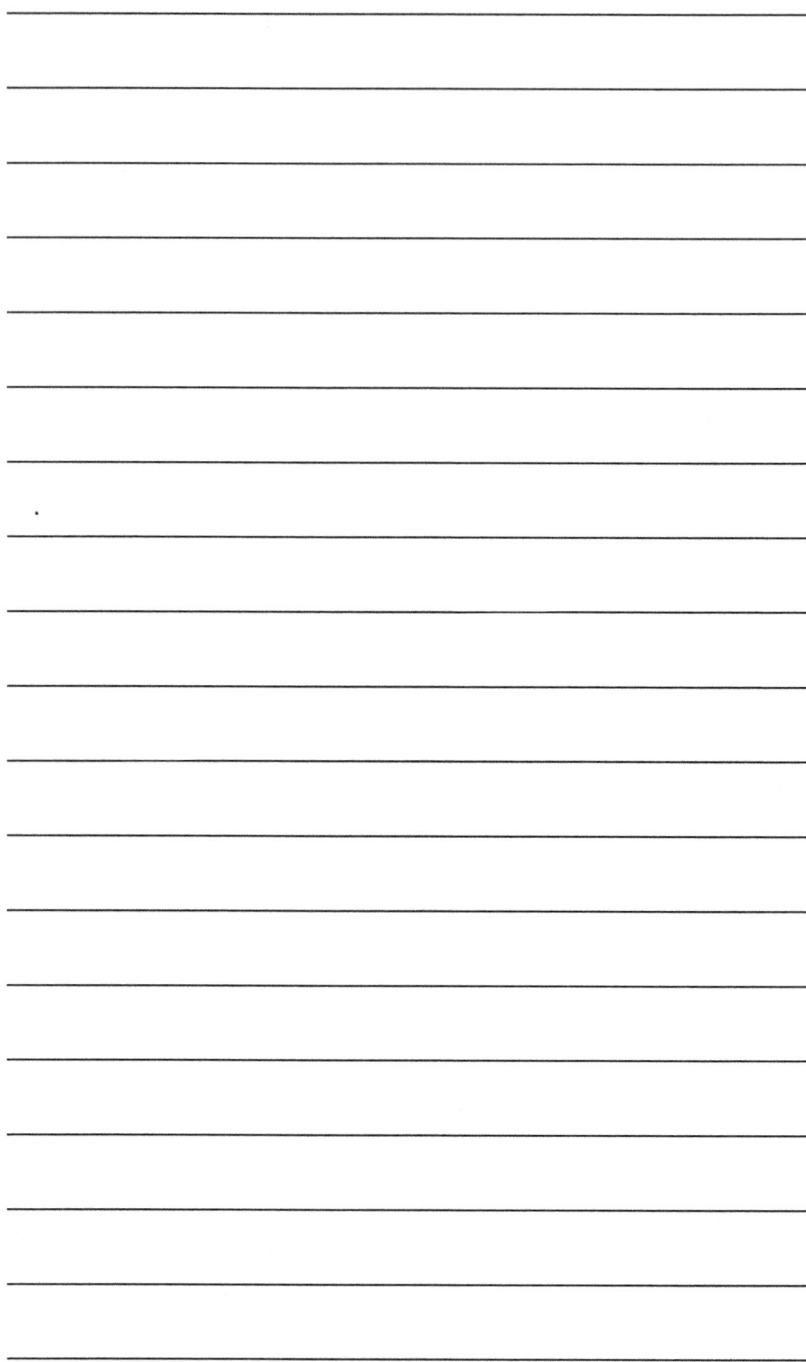

Bibliography and Essential Readings for Further Study

Anderson, Herbert, and Edward Foley. *Mighty Stories, Dangerous Rituals: Weaving Together the Human and the Divine*. San Francisco CA: Jossey-Bass Publishers, 1998.

Capps, Donald. *The Decades of Life: A Guide to Human Development*. Louisville KY: Westminster John Knox Press, 2008.

Chesnut, Mary Boykin Miller. *A Diary in Dixie*, edited by Isabella D. Martin and Myrta Lockett Avary. New York: D. Appleton & Co., 1905. Page 396. Electronic edition: Chapel Hill: University of North Carolina at Chapel Hill, 1997, http://docsouth.unc.edu/southlit/chesnut/maryches.html.

Buechner, Frederick. *Wishful Thinking: A Seeker's ABC*. New York: HarperOne, 1973.

Claypool, John. *Stages, the Art of Living the Expected*. Waco TX: Word Publishers, 1977.

Collins, Billy. "Aristotle," from *Picnic Lightning*. Pittsburgh: University of Pittsburgh Press, 1998.

Conroy, Pat. *The Prince of Tides*. New York: Houghton-Mifflin, 1986.

Coward, Nöel. "Nothing Is Lost." *Nöel Coward Collected Verse*. London UK: Methuen Publishing, Ltd., 2000.

"Death Expert Is Facing Her Own." AP. *Arizona Republic*. 19 October 2002.

Dickens, Charles. *A Tale of Two Cities*. In *The Works of Charles Dickens, Complete Edition*. New York: Oxford University Press American Branch, 1908.

Dillard, Annie. *For the Time Being.* New York: Alfred A. Knopf, Inc., 1999.

Erikson, Erik. *Dimensions of a New Identity.* New York: W. W. Norton and Co., 1974.

———. *Identity and the Life Cycle.* New York: International Universities Press, 1959.

Fulghum, Robert. *From Beginning to End: The Rituals of our Lives.* New York: Villard Books, 1995.

Griffith, J., and Powers, R. L. *The Lexicon of Adlerian Psychology: 106 Terms Associated with the Individual Psychology of Alfred Adler.* 2nd edition. Port Townsend WA: Adlerian Psychology Associates, 2007.

Hester, Richard L., and Kelli Walker-Jones. *Know Your Story and Lead with It: The Power of Narrative in Clergy Leadership.* Herndon VA: The Alban Institute, 2009.

Hester, Richard L., presenter. "Constructing Hopeful Narratives." The Oates Institute, Louisville KY, 1998.

Hillman, James. *The Soul's Code: In Search of Character and Calling.* New York: Random House, 1996.

Hogue, David A. *Remembering the Future, Imagining the Past: Story, Ritual, and the Human Brain.* Cleveland OH: The Pilgrim Press, 2003.

Hollis, James. *Finding Meaning in the Second Half of Life.* New York: Gotham Books, 2006.

Hoover, Paul. "Theory of Margins." *Chicago Review* vol. 47/48, no. 4/1 (Winter 2001).

Irving, John. *Cider House Rules.* New York: William Morrow and Company, Inc., 1985.

Johnson, Robert, with Jerry Ruhl. *Balancing Heaven and Earth, a Memoir.* New York: HarperCollins, 1998.

Jones, James W. *In the Middle of This Road We Call Our Life: The Courage to Search for Something More.* San Francisco CA: HarperSanFrancisco, 1997.

Kierkegaard, Søren. *The Journals of Søren Kierkegaard,* a selection edited and translated by Alexander Dru. London England: Oxford University Press, 1932.

Kübler-Ross, Elisabeth. *On Death and Dying: What the Dying Have to Teach Doctors, Nurses, Clergy and Their Own Families.* New York: Scribner's, 1969.

Loder, James E. *The Transforming Moment: Understanding Convictional Experiences.* New York: Harper and Row, Publishers, 1981.

Lynch, Thomas. *The Undertaking: Life Studies from the Dismal Trade.* New York: Penguin Books, 1997.

Madden, Myron C. *The Power to Bless: Healing and Wholeness through Understanding.* Nashville: Abingdon Press, 1970.

Márquez, Gabriel García. *Living to Tell the Tale*, translated from the Spanish by Edith Grossman. New York: Alfred A. Knopf, 2003.

———. *One Hundred Years of Solitude*, translated from the Spanish by Gregory Rabassa. New York: Harper and Row, 1970.

McMurtry, Larry. *Duane's Depressed*. New York: Simon and Schuster, 1999.

Monk, Gerald, John Winslade, Kathie Crockett, David Epstein, editors. *Narrative Therapy in Practice: The Archaeology of Hope*. San Francisco: Jossey-Bass Publishers, 1997.

Oliver, Mary. "The Summer Day." *New and Selected Poems*. Boston: Beacon Press, 1992.

Palmer, Parker. *A Hidden Wholeness: The Journey Toward an Undivided Life (Welcoming the soul and weaving community in a wounded world)*. San Francisco: Jossey-Bass, A Wiley Imprint, 2004.

Pipher, Mary. *Reviving Ophelia: Saving the Selves of Adolescent Girls*. New York: Ballantine Books, 1994.

Randall, William Lowell. *The Stories We Are: An Essay on Self-Creation*. Toronto Canada: University of Toronto Press, 1995.

Rohr, Richard. *Falling Upward: A Spirituality for the Two Halves of Life*. San Francisco: Jossey-Bass, 2011.

Schacter, Daniel L., editor. *Searching for Memory: The Brain, the Mind, and the Past*. New York: Basic Books, 1996.

Sheehy, Gail. *New Passages: Mapping Your Life Across Time*. New York: Ballantine Books, 1995.

Smith, Stevie. *Collected Poems of Stevie Smith*. New York: New Directions Publishing Corporation, 1972.

Stagg, Frank. *Polarities of Man's Existence in Biblical Perspective*. Philadelphia: Westminster Press, 1978.

Taylor, Barbara Brown. *God's Medicine*. Boston: Cowley Publications, 1995.

Tournier, Paul. *The Seasons of Life*. New York: Pillar Books, 1976.

Ware, Browning. *Austin American Statesman*. 20 August 2002.

White, M., and D. Epston. *Narrative Means to Therapeutic Ends*. New York: W.W. Norton, 1990.

Winnicott, D. W. *The Child, the Family, and the Outside World*. Reading MA: Addison-Wesley Publishing Co. Inc., 1964.

Endnotes

1. Lao Tzu, Tao Te Ching, trans. Stephen Mitchell (New York: Harper-Collins, 1988) 21.

2. Richard L. Hester & Kelli Walker-Jones, *Know Your Story and Lead with It: The Power of Narrative in Clergy Leadership* (Herndon VA: The Alban Institute, 2009).

3. Parker Palmer, *A Hidden Wholeness: The Journey Toward an Undivided Life* (San Francisco: Jossey-Bass, A Wiley Imprint, 2004) 115ff.

4. Narrative therapy resources will expand how this tool might be used. Refer to Gerald Monk et al., eds., *Narrative Therapy in Practice: The Archaeology of Hope* (San Francisco CA: Jossey-Bass Publishers, 1997) 250, for a description of this technique.

5. Hester and Walker-Jones, *Know Your Story*, 143–45.

6. Robert Fulghum, *From Beginning to End: The Rituals of our Lives* (New York: Villard Books, 1995) 20.

7. "Liminal," Merriam-Webster Dictionary, https://www.merriam-webster.com/dictionary/liminal.

8. The term "arc of life" broadly indicates how we can consider our lives from beginning to end, as Robert Fulghum defines it in his book, *From Beginning to End: The Rituals of our Lives* (New York: Villard Books, 1995). People who live the full range of life move through indefinite stages from birth until death in later adulthood, unless their lives are cut short—although even then the arc of life is merely abbreviated. The range of the arc of life would include our whole beings: every event, every emotion, every struggle, and every success.

9. For much of the past decade, Steve and I have been hosting narrative leadership workshops for ministers and leaders in which participants explore prescribed stories in a group process. Through this experience, they can see more clearly some aspects of their leadership and identify how they lead.

10. Anne Lamott, *Bird by Bird: Some Instructions on Writing and Life* (New York: Anchor Books, 1994) 5.

11. Gabriel García Márquez, *One Hundred Years of Solitude*, trans. Gregory Rabassa (New York: Harper and Row, 1970) 48.

12. Morris West, *The Clowns of God*, author's note (New York: William Morrow and Company, 1981) opening page.

13. A narrative community could be any small group that gathers for the purpose of exploring their stories.

14. James E. Loder, *The Transforming Moment: Understanding Convictional Experiences* (New York: Harper and Row, Publishers, 1981).

15. "Slender threads" is how Robert Johnson describes those capricious forces that affect how life is lived. He says, "Whether called fate, destiny, or the hand of God, slender threads are at work bringing coherence and continuity to our lives. Over time they weave a remarkable tapestry." Such forces sometimes appear to be happenstance while others appear, or at least are interpreted to be, actions guided by God, or one's answer to the activity of a larger hand" (Robert A. Johnson with Jerry M. Ruhl, *Balancing Heaven and Earth, a Memoir of Visions, Dreams, and Realizations* [New York: HarperCollins, 1998] xi).

16. Barbara Brown Taylor, *God's Medicine* (Boston, MA: Cowley Publications, 1995) 119–20.

17. Robert Johnson with Jerry Ruhl, *Between Heaven and Earth: A Memoir* (New York: HarperCollins, 1998).

18. Forrest Church, *The Cathedral of the World: A Universalist Theology* (Boston: Beacon Press, 2009) 5.

19. Donald Capps, *The Decades of Life: A Guide to Human Development* (Louisville, KY: Westminster John Knox Press, 2008).

20. Thomas Lynch, *The Undertaking: Life Studies from the Dismal Trade* (New York: Penguin Books, 1997) 24.

21. Herbert Anderson and Edward Foley, *Mighty Stories, Dangerous Rituals: Weaving Together the Human and the Divine* (San Francisco: Jossey-Bass Publishers, 1998) 22.

22. Robert Fulghum, *From Beginning to End: The Rituals of our Lives* (New York: Villard Books 1995) 20.

23. Frederick Buechner, *Now and Then* (New York: Harper & Row, Publishers, 1983) 92.

24. Ibid., 2–3.

25. Gabriel Garcia Marquez, *Living to Tell the Tale*, trans. Edith Grossman (New York: Alfred A. Knopf, 2003) opening page.

26. In Daniel L. Schacter, ed., *Searching for Memory: The Brain, the Mind, and the Past* (New York: Basic Books, 1996) 66.

27. David A. Hogue, *Remembering the Future, Imagining the Past: Story, Ritual, and the Human Brain* (Cleveland: The Pilgrim Press, 2003).

28. Ibid., 60–61.

29. Schacter, *Searching for Memory*, 66.

30. Richard L. Hester, presenter, "Constructing Hopeful Narratives," The Oates Institute, Louisville, KY, 1998.

31. William Lowell Randall, *The Stories We Are: An Essay on Self-Creation* (Toronto, Canada: University of Toronto Press, 1995) 57–58.

32. Mary Boycut Miller Chesnut, *A Diary in Dixie*, ed. Isabella D. Martin and Myrta Lockett Avary (New York: D. Appleton & Co., 1905) 396, electronic edition owned by the University of North Carolina at Chapel Hill, 1997, http://docsouth.unc.edu/southlit/chesnut/maryches.html.

33. M. White and D. Epston, *Narrative Means to Therapeutic Ends* (New York: W.W. Norton, 1990) 11–12.

34. More information on this re-authoring process is given in Essay One, "How to Use This Book."

35. Paul Hoover, "Theory of Margins," *Chicago Review*, vol. 47/48, no. 4/1 (Winter 2001): 205

36. "The contract of life" is a concept that helps me understand how all the factors mentioned in this essay are important realities that make up the challenge of life. "The contract of life" is a rough estimation of

the cumulative effects of DNA and of being born in a certain culture, a certain time in history, and in a certain location. Social location; the attitudes of our parents toward the values they live; their attitudes toward reading, school, work; their view of others who are different from them; and a million other factors give definition to how we will engage the challenge of our own lives. What we do with all these factors will determine what our lives will be.

37. Gerald Monk, John Winslade, Kathie Crockett, David Epstein, eds., *Narrative Therapy in Practice: The Archaeology of Hope* (San Francisco: Jossey-Bass, 1997) 3.

38. Scholars of memory catalogue different types of memory by determining how each one functions in relation to the information it holds. There are two basic types of memory: working memory and long-term memory. Within those types are sub-categories of memory such as semantic memory, procedural memory, and autobiographical memory. The brain stores bits of information in different areas but reassembles needed information for the purpose of memory.

39. "Slender threads" is a particular phrase coined by psychotherapist Robert Johnson in his memoir, *Balancing Heaven and Earth* (New York: HarperCollins, 1998, p. 1) as a metaphorical phrase to explain how certain things may happen in life to shape and mold us. These can be apparent happenstance, what we would call good fortune or even luck. They can be tragic or devastating. The interruption of how life is being lived is at the heart of slender threads, and it may or may not be considered as a sign of the action of some larger being directing one's life, depending on one's view of faith. Certainly all these factors are in the eye of the beholder and interpreted according to one's perspective.

40. Frank Stagg, *Polarities of Man's Existence in Biblical Perspective* (Louisville KY: Westminster Press, 1978) 75, citing Abraham Heschel, *Who Is Man?* (Redwood City CA: Stanford University Press, 1965) 44ff.

41. Psalm 91:4-6, NRSV.

42. Grady Nutt, *Being Me.*

43. J. Griffith and R. L. Powers, *The Lexicon of Adlerian Psychology: 106 Terms Associated with the Individual Psychology of Alfred Adler*, 2nd ed. (Port Townsend WA: Adlerian Psychology Associates, 2007) 26

44. Ibid., 185

45. John Claypool, *Stages: The Art of Living the Expected* (Waco TX: Word Publishers, 1977) 21–25.

46. Myron C. Madden, *The Power to Bless: Healing and Wholeness through Understanding* (Nashville: Abingdon Press, 1970) 141.

47. Conception through coitus is the common method for reproduction to occur. This writer acknowledges that medical science has achieved the displacement of sexual processes and replaced it with what I call "high-tech sex."

48. Pat Conroy, *The Prince of Tides* (New York: Houghton-Mifflin, 1986) 85–86.

49. D. W. Winnicott, *The Child, the Family, and the Outside World* (Reading MA: Addison-Wesley Publishing Co. Inc., 1964) 173.

50. Story told by John Claypool, "To Live Is to Improvise," sermon, Northminster Baptist Church, Jackson MS, 11 June 1978.

51. Donald Capps, *The Decades of Life: A Guide to Human Development* (Louisville KY: Westminster John Knox Press, 2008) 32.

52. Erik Erikson, *Identity and the Life Cycle* (New York: International Universities Press, 1959) 52.

53. Søren Kierkegaard, *The Journals of Søren Kierkegaard*, a selection edited and translated by Alexander Dru (London: Oxford University Press, 1932) 1:1030.

54. 1 Corinthians 13:11, NRSV.

55. Erikson, *Identity*, 66.

56. Ibid., 68.

57. Mary Pipher, *Reviving Ophelia: Saving the Selves of Adolescent Girls* (New York: Ballantine Books, 1994) 20.

58. Stevie Smith, "Not Waving but Drowning," in *Collected Poems of Stevie Smith* (New York: New Directions Publishing Corporation, 1972). Also at https://www.poetryfoundation.org/poems/46479/not-waving-but-drowning.

59. Pipher, *Reviving Ophelia*, 43.

60. Wendell Berry, lecture given at the Stetson Winter Pastors' School, 2013.

61. John Irving, *Cider House Rules* (New York: William Morrow and Company, Inc., 1985) 87–88.

62. This and the quotes below are from James Hillman, *The Soul's Code: In Search of Character and Calling* (New York: Random House, 1996) 27ff.

63. Those who are steeped in the language and imagery of early mythologies understand Hillman's use of *daimon* to mean fate or calling.

64. Ralph Keyes, *Is There Life after High School?* (New York: Little, Brown & Co., 1976).

65. Richard Rohr, *Falling Upward: A Spirituality for the Two Halves of Life* (San Francisco: Jossey-Bass, 2011) 1.

66. John Claypool, *Stages: The Art of Living the Expected* (Waco TX: Word Publishers, 1977) 59–60.

67. Claypool, *Stages*, 61.

68. Robert Johnson with Jerry Ruhl, *Between Heaven and Earth: A Memoir* (New York: HarperCollins, 1998) 1.

69. Rohr, *Falling Up*, xix.

70. James Hollis, *Finding Meaning in the Second Half of Life* (New York: Gotham Books, 2006) 100–101.

71. Ibid., 122–23.

72. Claypool, *Stages*, 81.

73. Larry McMurtry's book series, known as the Thalia stories (*The Last Picture Show, Texasville, Duane's Depressed, When the Light Goes*, and *Rhino Ranch*), all follow the same characters developed in the first novel and illustrate key developmental stages in the life of oil driller Duane Moore.

74. Larry McMurtry, *Duane's Depressed* (New York: Simon and Schuster, 1999) 133.

75. For a complete discussion of these two concepts, see Hollis, *Finding Meaning in the Second Half of Life*, 182ff.

76. James W. Jones, *In the Middle of this Road We Call Our Life: The Courage to Search for Something More* (San Francisco: HarperSanFrancisco, 1997) 1.

77. Mary Oliver, "The Summer Day," *New and Selected Poems* (Boston: Beacon Press, 1992) 94.

78. Frederick Buechner, *Wishful Thinking: A Seeker's ABC* (New York: HarperOne, 1973) 118–19.

79. Hollis, *Finding Meaning in the Second Half of Life*, 182–83.

80. Ibid., inside cover.

81. Thanks to Browning Ware for inspiration of these thoughts about the readiness for the approach of death in his column in the *Austin American Statesman*, 20 August 2002.

82. Paul Tournier, *The Seasons of Life* (New York: Pillar Books, 1976) 46–47.

83. Ibid., 54–55.

84. Erik Erikson, *Dimensions of a New Identity* (New York: W. W. Norton and Co., 1974) 124.

85. Erik Erikson, *Identity and the Life Cycle* (New York: International Universities Press, 1959) 98.

86. Charles Dickens, *A Tale of Two Cities*, in *The Works of Charles Dickens*, Complete Edition (New York: Oxford University Press American Branch, 1908) 347.

87. John Claypool, *Stages: The Art of Living the Expected* (Waco TX: Word Publishers, 1977) 81.

88. Elisabeth Kübler-Ross, *On Death and Dying: What the Dying Have to Teach Doctors, Nurses, Clergy & Their Own Families* (New York: Scribner's, 1969).

89. "Death Expert Is Facing Her Own," AP, *Arizona Republic*, 19 October 2002.

90. Paul Tournier, *The Seasons of Life* (New York: Pillar Books, 1976) 54.

91. Ibid., 50–51.

92. Nöel Coward, "Nothing Is Lost," *Nöel Coward Collected Verse* (London UK: Methuen Publishing, Ltd., 2000) 66.

93. Psalm 90:1-5, NRSV.

94. Annie Dillard, *For the Time Being* (New York: Alfred A. Knopf, Inc., 1999) 157–58.

95. Robert Fulghum, *From Beginning to End: The Rituals of our Lives* (New York: Villard Books, 1995) vi.

96. Forrester Church, *The Cathedral of the World: A Universalist Theology* (Boston: Beacon Press, 2009) 168–69.

Index